Bits and Pieces

Books by Whoopi Goldberg

Whoopi Goldberg

Bits and Pieces

MY MOTHER, MY BROTHER, AND ME

BLACK
STONE
PUBLISHING

Printed in the United States of America

First edition: 2024
ISBN 979-8-200-92023-5
Biography & Autobiography / Personal Memoirs

Version 1

Blackstone Publishing
31 Mistletoe Rd.
Ashland, OR 97520

www.BlackstonePublishing.com

This book is for everyone who knew my mother and brother.

Introduction

Probably none of us had the childhoods we think we had. We only have our individual memories of what we believe happened. You can talk to siblings born two years apart, and they will give you different perspectives on the same event or experience in their childhoods.

So, what's that supposed to mean? We can't trust our memories? You know, yeah. That's exactly what it means.

When my mother died unexpectedly in August 2010, it took me a while to feel the full effect of her being gone. I still had my older brother, Clyde. As long as he was with me, I had my home base. There were only the three of us in my family: Mother, Brother, and me. I knew Clyde and I would be okay. We were both in our fifties, so I thought I'd have my brother in my life for at least another twenty-five years.

Then, five years after my mom passed, Clyde suddenly died of an aneurysm. I was stunned by it, but
not really surprised in a way. He was different after our
mom died. Losing her was devastating beyond words for
Clyde, more than he could share with me. When she
died, a large part of my brother disappeared with her.
Most people couldn't see it, but I did.

After Clyde died, I didn't know what to do with
myself. I wasn't ready to feel so alone. Being an orphan
hit me much harder. I wanted to crawl into a cave and hole
up. But my work schedule wouldn't allow for it. I carried
on . . . feeling flat. That's all I could do. I couldn't kick and
scream or stomp my feet. That would change nothing.

Suddenly I felt there might be many loose ends and
unanswered questions. But, at the same time, I had no
proof that there were loose ends to resolve. I began to
doubt if any of my memories were real, or if they were
something I saw or read a long time ago.

Clyde was the only brain I had on my memories, the
only witness to my growing-up years.

I used to ask him, "Am I crazy? Did this really
happen?"

And he'd say something like, "It happened, Sis, but
it was during this time or that time." Or, "We did go
there during that time, and here's why . . ."

Now, I no longer have Clyde to set me straight. I have no one left to ask.

It's this thing we all have to face, the death of those who knew you the best, the people in your life story. I am very lonely for my family. I get lonely for the two of them.

I really should start this book by saying it's possible that nothing in this book happened, or it's possible that nothing I have written in this book happened the way I say it did. I never kept journals or datebooks. I don't know the calendar year for many of my memories or even my age at the time.

You might be asking, "Why are you writing a memoir, then?"

Because the two most magnificent people I've ever known were my mother, Emma, and my brother, Clyde, and they had almost everything to do with how I became the person I am.

Also, I can sense that my memories of my mom, which used to fire strong like a torch, have now become more of a flicker in the thirteen years since she passed away. I know the same will happen with Clyde, so I want to put them down in words before they fade further.

In addition to all the great roles I've played in movies, TV, and on stage, in character or as myself over the years,

I've also done a lot of writing. I've written solo shows, comedy sketches, songs, host monologues for the Oscars, storybooks for kids, a black girl's *Alice in Wonderland*, and published books about relationships, aging, political and social issues, and even manners.

Now it's time for a book about my nucleus family: my brother, Clyde, and especially about my mother, because none of the other stuff would have happened for me without her. I never doubted that she loved me for exactly who I was. My mom made me believe I could do anything I wanted. When I told her that I thought that would be acting, she listened, had conversations with me about it, and backed me up. Because of my mom, I was able to go from being Caryn Johnson, the "little weird kid" from the projects who no one ever expected to achieve all that much, to being me, Whoopi Goldberg.

I know how lucky I was and am. Not everybody gets to walk this earth with folks who let you be exactly who you are and who give you the confidence to become exactly who you want to be. So, I thought I'd share mine with you.

Chapter One

My mother, Emma Johnson, and my brother, Clyde, were already a lockstep duo by the time I showed up on the scene. Clyde was six, and nobody knew how old my mother was. She refused to tell her age to me or anybody. Still, I tried to get it out of her once in a while. I'm not sure why. She was notorious for answering my questions with a question.

"Why do you want to know?" she would say.

"Because it's your birthday," I'd answer. "So, how old are you?"

"Why does it matter?"

"I'd just like to know."

She would light a Kool cigarette and give me a look.

"I'm old enough to be your mother."

That's as far as I'd get.

As a kid, I tried not to annoy my mom by asking too many questions. In the 1960s, adults didn't think kids should know their business, at least not in my neighborhood.

It wasn't until I was in my fifties that she told me a secret she had kept for forty years, and it gave me a lot more insight into why she was the way she was and how I got to be the way I am.

I thought my mother was the most interesting, beautiful, funny, and wise person in the world. And Clyde was the coolest sibling anybody could possibly have. I felt that way as a kid, and it never changed. I knew I was lucky that my mom and Clyde allowed me to hang with them. It's not like they didn't want me to be around. They had bonded in this magical nucleus of two, which they expanded to include me.

The three of us lived in the Chelsea projects at Twenty-Sixth Street and Tenth Avenue in Manhattan, in a five-room apartment on the sixth floor of a twelve-story brick building. There were nine other buildings that matched ours. We had about 2,400 close neighbors. Lots of folks of every color, religion, language, and culture, all packed into a couple of city blocks.

Apparently, we lived in the projects because we were poor, but I didn't know it. When you're a little kid, you accept the way things are. Nobody told me what "poor" meant because everyone around me was in the same situation. I lived among a whole lot of people barely getting by. Somehow, my mom made my brother and me feel like we lived at the entrance gate of a big, interesting world in which we could do anything we wanted to do.

From as early on as I remember, my mother would say to me, "Listen. The confines of this neighborhood do not represent the confines of your life. You can go and do and be whatever you want. But, whatever you choose, be yourself."

I believed her. That's what made the real difference in my future.

In reality, there was no extra cash, no rainy-day fund, no spare-change jar on top of the fridge. No child support checks came in the mail. No inheritance would be forthcoming. My mother's mom had died at age fifty, and her father had remarried. Nothing was expected in a will. Emma was on her own, except she wasn't. She had Clyde and me.

Even when I asked her, well into my adult years, "Ma, how did you take us to see the Ice Capades and the Christmas Spectacular at Radio City Music Hall and all the other experiences we had?"

She'd answer, "Why are you asking me that?"

I'd say, "Because we always went everywhere and saw everything. How did you do that? How did you make that happen?"

"I have no idea why you're asking me that," she'd say.

I'd end up feeling kind of foolish, like I wasn't asking in the right way. So I'd drop it. It was a mystery to me then, and now that she's gone, it always will be.

New York City in the 1960s and '70s was the hub of it all. Everything was going on: pop art, timeless art, classical ballet, the symphony, protest music, Alvin Ailey dancers, beatnik poets, street theater, hippies, civil rights, women's lib, gay rights, Lincoln Center Theater, film, Miles Davis, Birdland, Joe Papp and Shakespeare in the Park, and a long line of high-kick dancing women at Radio City Music Hall. Everything was a fifteen-cent bus or subway ride away, ten cents for kids.

My mother would figure out which days were free at the galleries and museums and make sure that Clyde and I were out the door to go see the newest exhibit at the Metropolitan Museum of Art or the American Museum of Natural History, even though she could rarely go with us because of her job.

At home, our tabletop record player played all types of music: Lady Day; Bing Crosby; Ella Fitzgerald;

Peter, Paul and Mary; Pavarotti; the Supremes; Sinatra; and the Beatles. My mother had an eye and ear for what she liked, and she liked the Beatles.

The Beatles played Shea Stadium in 1965. My mother had somehow scored tickets. Our seats were way up high, along the top rim of the stadium. Huge floodlights buzzed right over our heads, but it didn't matter. We were in the stadium with fifty-six thousand other fans. Not many other nine-year-old kids were in that crowd, watching four guys from England in matching jackets and black pants sing "Can't Buy Me Love," but my mom made it happen for me.

For some reason, she wasn't a fan of the Rolling Stones' music and didn't want it played in the house. I think I remember her saying something about them "being dirty." I thought she meant unbathed, but it was probably about the lyrics. My mother rarely said anything negative about anybody. She thought "(I Can't Get No) Satisfaction" and "Get Off of My Cloud" were not as sweet as "I Want to Hold Your Hand."

There wasn't much room for complaining when I was growing up. My mother would say, "If you're going to feel bad today, then make it big. Lie on the couch and throw your wrist across your forehead and sigh loudly, so we all know what's going on for you. That way we can step back and say, 'Okay. That's what she's doing now. Go ahead. Get it over with. I'll wait.'"

She did not believe in self-pity. Her attitude was simple, and one of the big things she put in my head was this: "You've got two choices. You can waste a lot of time complaining, or you can get up and figure out how to fix it."

My mother was clear: "I have to be practical. I have two kids. I can't spend a lot of time crying about what I don't have. I have to figure out what I do have and go from there." That was her approach. She didn't complain or explain. However, my mother laughed. A lot. She loved a good reason to laugh. Clyde and I got the same gene. The three of us knew how to have a good time together.

When I was about eight, my mother, brother, and I took a subway and maybe a bus to Rockaways' Playland amusement park. That kind of adventure was always a treat day. The park had a fun house entrance, a giant barrel that rotated slowly on its side, and you had to walk through as it spun to the side under your feet.

Clyde made it through, no problem. I crossed through next. Then, we heard my mother's laugh. We looked back into the barrel and saw her on her hands and knees, trying to keep from tipping over as the barrel turned.

Whenever she tried to stand up again, she would laugh harder and fall back to the floor.

Clyde inched back in to give her a hand up and ended up on his ass, too. So, you know, I thought I'd better get back in there and join them. The three of us tumbled from side to side, Clyde and me screaming with laughter and my mother's light musical laugh bouncing around in the barrel.

Eventually, a carnival worker turned the whole thing off, hoping to get this crazy family out of there.

As a little kid, I always felt secure and loved. I thought everything would come out okay because my mom was in charge. Between her and Clyde and me, I thought we could do anything.

It wasn't until I was older that I really understood what my mother had to go through to keep a roof over our heads. My father and mother had separated, so I didn't grow up with him. She tried to get him to pay some support through the courts, but helping black women living in the projects wasn't high on the state court's priority list, and she couldn't afford a lawyer who might have gotten something done.

Still, she refused to apply for welfare, saying, "If I am able to work and take care of my own, then I should do that." She didn't like the stigma of being on welfare.

I saw her cry once or twice about being unable to pay her taxes. But as a kid, I never grasped that we were always one paycheck away from the worst-case scenario.

Kind of like the fun house barrel, my mother never got to stand still for a minute and let someone else handle it all for a while. No one was going to show up and rescue her, and she knew it. There was no alternative plan to fall back on. Whatever challenges she had to face, she somehow managed. And she did it alone.

Clyde and I never thought she needed rescuing. She had an air of authority. We didn't question it. But in reality, she had to endure a whole lot of stuff that would've beaten down somebody with less backbone.

In 1994, eight years after I starred in the movie *Jumpin' Jack Flash*, I called my mom up to ask her a question.

"Ma, the Rolling Stones want me to come to Miami for the filming of their Voodoo Lounge Tour, introduce them to the crowd, and then join them onstage when they perform 'Jumpin' Jack Flash.' Do you want to go with me?"

I wasn't sure how she'd answer, considering how she'd felt about them during my childhood, but she told me she'd like to attend.

When I joined Mick Jagger on stage for "Jumpin'

Jack Flash," I looked down from the stage to see my mother up and dancing in the front row, holding her cigarette lighter high above her head. (Back then, we didn't have cell phones to wave around, so lighters held by thousands of fans had to do.) I couldn't take my eyes off her—my mother having a great time rockin' to the Stones.

I looked at her and started laughing. She looked back at me and laughed. That's how we did life, right up to the day she died.

Chapter Two

I was still wearing a head-to-toe nun's habit when I got a call from my brother, Clyde. He was at my house in Berkeley, California. I was in London, performing in the stage version of *Sister Act* at the Palladium in August 2010.

My regular gig, hosting *The View*, was on a month-long hiatus, so off I went to the West End to do a limited run of twenty shows. This time, I was playing Mother Superior instead of the role I originated in the 1992 movie, cabaret star Deloris Van Cartier. I was fifty-four now, so I figured the chief nun was a better fit.

I had two shows left before heading home.

Actress Maggie Smith and some of her friends were at the show that night to see me. She had come back-stage to my dressing room to say hello and talk, which

I loved. When my phone rang and I saw it was Clyde, I thought I'd be telling him I'd call him back.

"It's Ma," Clyde said.

"What d'ya mean? What's goin' on?" I asked.

"Caryn, Ma died. A couple hours ago."

"How? Where?"

Clyde told me that she had asked him to go to the store for a newspaper and some More cigarettes. She loved smoking More cigarettes and never wanted to run out of them. When he got back, he found her sideways on the couch with an unlit cigarette in her hand, smiling, but she wasn't breathing.

"She's at the hospital," Clyde told me. "But listen, she's gone."

I could hear in Clyde's voice that he was pretty shook up. Neither one of us expected anything like this. The doctor told Clyde that it was an aneurysm.

He was feeling awful, like he could have saved her. But that didn't seem to be the case, according to the doctor. A blood vessel had exploded in her brain. She went quickly. Here one minute, gone the next.

I've got to say, if there's one family trait that we all shared, it's efficiency. We get down to business.

I had been on a FaceTime call with my mom the day before. We had talked about the grandkids, rose bushes, cats, dogs, and Clyde. We had laughed for an hour. She'd seemed fine.

FaceTime had just come out. At first, my mother thought she didn't want to bother with it. She was fine with regular talking on the phone. But once I showed her how easy it was, she got into it. Even though I was five thousand miles away, we could still have eyes on each other every day.

I talked to my mom on the phone almost every day of my adult life when I wasn't with her in person. Every conversation always ended the same way. My mother, brother, and I always told each other everything we thought the other person should know before we hung up. If we had any problems with the others, we'd get it out and be done with it. One of us would say, "Is there anything else you think I should know? Anything else going on?" And we'd end every call with "I love you." We always did that, I guess, as a "just-in-case."

I couldn't wrap my head around the fact that the "just-in-case" was for real this time.

"What will the hospital do now?" I asked my brother. I wanted to see her.

"I asked them to leave her on support until you can get home," Clyde told me.

He wanted to make sure I had a chance to say my farewells and kiss her goodbye.

"I'll get on the first plane I can find," I told him.

"Don't rush. She's not here anymore. It's okay, Sis."

I explained to Maggie Smith what was going on and apologized for having to fly home as soon as I could. I'm sure I was walking around in a dazed circle.

That's when this magnificent woman, Dame Maggie Smith, went from being my backstage company to being my friend through the rest of the night. She decided she would stay with me until I was on my way to the airport. A flight was arranged for me to leave early the next morning. For the next five hours, Maggie sat with me and let me talk her ear off, telling stories about my mom, my growing-up years, and my brother. We laughed a lot.

I don't know if I was in shock. I had never been in shock before. I don't think I cried. I didn't feel anything except a big wave of kindness from Maggie. I've got to say, she is one of those people for whom I would do anything. Anything Maggie Smith needs, I got her covered.

I went straight from the airport in San Francisco to the hospital, knowing that my post-Mom life was now starting. She had prepared me for this day, but I would never be ready. I wasn't ready to not be her kid.

My mom was in a hospital gown, lying in the bed, with the ventilator running. She looked peaceful, not in any pain.

Clyde and I agreed to pull the plug together, turning off life support. The room went silent. And then this nucleus that had been the three of us became the two of us. When I looked at Clyde's face, his eyes looked empty, like he was gone, too.

We stood by her bed, silent for some time.

I asked Clyde if he knew what was supposed to happen next. We were told that a mortuary should be called to pick up her body. There was important stuff to discuss.

"Do you know what Ma wanted?" Clyde asked.

I said, "I might know. Remember when the three of us were talking about someone who passed recently? Ma had said, 'I don't want to be put in the ground and take up space. I don't want people to feel they have to come visit. Just put me in the microwave.'"

Like I said: efficient.

Clyde kind of remembered that being her attitude. Now, we had to figure out how that could happen. Was a huge microwave an actual thing? We started making phone calls. The first two funeral homes we called acted like, "What the fuck? No, we don't have a giant microwave! And as a matter of fact . . . no one does."

Then, the third one we called said, "Our microwave is broken down, but come and see us and we will do our best to take care of you."

Off we went to see this place that wasn't afraid to help us out. It seemed they understood folks in grief who had never had to deal with the death of someone close before.

In the front lobby of the mortuary, Clyde said to the director, "We are going to need . . ."

The man finished his sentence and said, ". . . a coffin. Come downstairs."

There were a bunch of coffins. My mother was clear about *not* wanting a funeral plot or a funeral, not wanting to be buried in the ground. That was only one of many decisions. Somehow, my brother and I did everything that was needed in order for the cremation.

Clyde and I sent some of her ashes to a whole bunch of folks that she loved, but the response wasn't too great. Most of them were pretty annoyed that we weren't having a memorial service. But Ma had made it clear that she didn't want that. She never wanted people to go out of their way or interrupt their plans or their day. As she had put it, "Memorials are for other people, not the dead person. It's not like I care. I'm not there, anyway. So, if you don't mind, I'd rather not."

In September, on what would have been her birthday, Clyde and I took most of her remaining ashes to Disneyland, one of her favorite places.

Disneyland was a place Ma always wanted to take Clyde and me as kids. Every Sunday night, we would watch *Walt Disney's Wonderful World of Color* on NBC. The opening titles had Tinker Bell flying across the screen and leaving splotches of color with her magic wand. I knew if my mom could've figured out how to get us three to Disneyland, we would've gone.

In the mid-1970s, when I was in my early twenties, I had some steadier jobs in San Diego. I saved enough money to buy a round-trip ticket for my mom to fly out from New York to see me. It took a while to get the cash together, but I had a plan in mind.

A day after she arrived, we got in the car and took off on the highway. We were driving along and talking for about an hour when she asked me, "Where are we going?"

"Oh, I'm looking for this park I heard about," I said casually. "It's probably coming up."

Somehow, she missed seeing the Disneyland sign that was on the exit I took.

After driving down Harbor Boulevard for a couple miles, she said, "Caryn, I'd really like to get out of this car now."

So, I said, "Let's pull in here. This looks like a good place to walk around."

I turned in on Disneyland Drive, and she looked

around, saw where we were, and burst into tears. My mom almost never cried, so I knew she was feeling it.

"I was supposed to do this for you and Clyde," she said, looking over at me.

"Ma, it doesn't matter who did it for who. We're here now. Come on, let's go see it."

I took her to everything in Disneyland. I bought us some Mickey ears, and we wore them around all day. We stood in lines, rode every ride we'd heard about, hugged the characters, and took in all the attractions. She was knocked out by it.

She especially loved the "Small World" ride. It was her vision of what human beings should be, these children of the world: all colors, religions, and cultures together. Disney had made it seem possible that all the kids of the world would hold hands in unity.

When we got off "It's a Small World," she told me again, "I wish I could have done this for you."

I didn't know if I'd ever be able to take her to Disneyland again. I hoped so, but who knew?

The day Clyde and I took her ashes to Disneyland, it's possible a lot of her went into the "Small World" ride, her favorite. We were subtle about it, kind of sneezing Ma out here and there when no one was looking. We didn't get caught, but I confessed it later to a park employee. They weren't surprised, and they certainly were not happy about it.

I later learned that it's pretty common and that a lot of family calcium phosphate has been scattered here and there in Disney parks. (The employees are seriously on the lookout for it now. I've been told it's a HEPA cleanup issue. You might find yourself escorted to the parking lot pretty quick. Don't do what I did. I'm sure you don't want your loved one's final resting place to be an industrial vacuum bag.)

It took a while to settle in on me that my mom's death has been the most devastating experience of my life. It was an acute trauma. I still think about her every single day.

My mother held her cards close to her vest. I didn't know much about her childhood until I was in my forties. Clyde and I must have caught her on a talkative day when she told us about growing up in Harlem.

My mom, Emma, was an only child, and her cousin, Arlene, was like her sister. The two of them lived with Emma's mom, Rachel, and Arlene's mom, Ruth, who were actual sisters. Their moms were as different as day and night. Ruth was a five-foot-tall force of nature. She carried around a small Louisville Slugger so her husband, Slim, listened to whatever she had to say. If there was a problem, Ruth and her Louisville had no issues kicking some man's ass.

Emma's mom, Rachel, was not as strong-willed. When her husband, Maliki, decided to leave the marriage, she knew she had to let him go. I think it was disappointing to my mom as a little girl. The split-up of her parents left a huge hole in her heart.

Ruth and Rachel raised their daughters like exact equals. What was given to one was given to the other. They had identical dresses and Polly II shoes, dolls and games, and got the same number of gifts under the Christmas tree so there would always be peace in the valley of Arlene and Emma. But they didn't look alike. At all. Arlene was a true redhead, with hair that fell in ringlets and light-skinned with freckles. She looked like a darling Shirley Temple doll.

My mom did not look like Shirley Temple. She was chocolate brown, all long legs and arms, with wide chocolate eyes. Not many relatives called her Emma. Folks would call her "Monk," short for monkey. When she told me that, I was pissed off. I wanted to get that Louisville Slugger and kick some ass of my own. What the fuck? How mean can you be to a kid?

My mother just shrugged as she told the story. It didn't seem to bother her, at least not anymore. She was more like an actual monk. She seemed completely able to embrace the golden rule: treat others the way you

want to be treated. That's the way she lived, despite a
lot of stuff she went through for the whole first half of
her life that could have made her resentful as hell, which
I found incredible.

Her dad married the "other" woman, a nice lady
named Margaret, who had an ice cream shop in Harlem.
They had one daughter together. When Emma visited
her half sister, dad, and stepmom, I think she felt unwel-
comed. It wasn't that anyone was mean or said anything
to her, but the climate had changed.

On Easter Sunday, as kids, my mother would make
sure Clyde and I were dressed up, and she'd take us on
an uptown bus to visit our grandfather and Margaret
in Harlem. The best part of the day was sitting at the
counter of her ice cream parlor to have a soda fountain
drink. My grandfather, who liked photography, took to
Clyde and taught him a love for taking pictures. I don't
remember him doing anything special with me. I think
in those days, attention was paid more to the males in
the family. I also do not remember it bothering me at
the time, so . . . there you are.

I do think my mom felt that same rejection from
him. Even after her father died and she was grown, she
felt that she was still treated like an outsider. Her father's family sorted through his belongings and decided

what my mother should be given. She was never asked what she would like to have. No one ever got in touch with us again until I became famous. Then they all reappeared. But my mom never spoke badly about any of them. She dealt with it.

My mom's saving grace as a girl was her grandmother, Emmaline, who loved everything about the movies. She would take her namesake along to see new releases at the local movie houses. My mom's first nine years of life were during the Depression, and movies at that time were affordable getaways from problems. The two of them would catch the first feature in the morning at 9:00 a.m. and then stay all day long until dinnertime. They'd see Clark Gable in *Too Hot to Handle*, Bette Davis in *Jezebel*, Charlie Chaplin movies, *The Philadelphia Story* with Hepburn and Grant, the first run of all the Abbott and Costello movies, Disney's original *Fantasia*, and *The Wizard of Oz* on the big screen. My mom became a fan of Judy Garland. The movies gave Emma a view of the bigger world and everything going on outside of her life in Harlem. They made her curious about other places and times in history, so she would check books out of the library to learn about it all. My great-grandmother was the only one in the family fascinated with showbiz, so I guess I inherited her genes.

Since Ma was on a roll, telling Clyde and me about her parents and grandparents, I thought I'd ask her more about our dad, Robert Johnson. But it was not a conversation she wanted to have. She was from the old school, where everything was on a need-to-know for kids and young adults. So I didn't get much information on that front, but here's what I surmise . . . my mom was on her own to raise the two of us.

My mother didn't talk about the marriage ending because she stayed married to him until the day he passed, nor do I think she ever thought of it as a failure. It turns out that my dad was gay. Which couldn't have been easy either.

I'm telling you, he had many gigs—he was a diamond merchant and spent time working in the post office. He was raised in a strict Southern Baptist household, and his mother, Hattie, was one of those ladies who wore the nurse uniform to the church service and revived the folks who fainted when they were overcome by the spirit.

Hattie was the one who helped my mother get an apartment in the projects when they were newly built because she might have known or worked for somebody who was organizing it all. I think about what those apartment buildings must have looked like when my mother first moved down to Chelsea from Harlem. I can't imagine what that relief must have been like for my mom, finding a place she would be able to afford where she could be with her family.

She made it really clear to Clyde and me that we needed to keep the apartment as clean as possible. I guess my mother thought if it was messy at all, it would reflect badly on my grandmother or some crazy shit like that.

Most of the families in our building worked their asses off to maintain their apartments because, in those days, people thought that folks who lived in the projects and were poor must be dirty. The city let the buildings get run-down, but the occupants did their best to keep their homes looking good because they didn't want the stereotype. When you read about the kind of insane racism in today's news, it's nothing that hasn't been here for a long time.

My father, being a gay black man, couldn't have had it easy in the 1960s. (Hell, it's still not easy.) In those days, you could still be thrown in jail if you were at a gay bar. I think he loved my mother, too, but couldn't stay in the marriage and be true to himself. I liked that about him, but he let my mother carry on alone as a single mom. Yet she never had a bad word to say about him.

I would only see him occasionally. He would have Clyde for a weekend once in a while. He definitely had more to say and do with his son than his daughter. Come to think of it, neither one of my parents ever filed for divorce. I think he was the love of my mom's life. She never dated or showed much interest in any other man that I know about.

When I was a kid, I'd ask her, "Ma, do you want a boyfriend?"

She'd say, "Do you think I need one?"

I'd say, "No, I don't think you *need* one, but do you want one?"

Then I would start to sweat because I was a little kid and I didn't actually know *why* she would want one. This was way before I understood what all that entailed. But I'd get to where there was no info coming from her and no more questions from me, so it would end in a stand-off. No boyfriend . . .

I do remember asking this about my father: "Ma, why doesn't he like me?"

She would say, "Of course he likes you. But he is who he is. And I can't answer that question. The next time you see him, you must ask him yourself."

One of my mom's pet peeves was when people wouldn't be direct about something. She thought people should answer for themselves and take responsibility for their choices and reasons. This was not one of my father's strong suits.

Still, I thought I'd see if she would answer one question that had to do with her. It was after my father passed away in 1993, so she couldn't tell me to ask him directly.

"When and how did you know he was gay?"

She lit her cigarette and said, "I never thought about it."

What that meant coming from my mom: *I know, but I'm not talking about it, and this conversation is now done.* It was another mystery, and it was going to stay a mystery.

Harvard professor Dr. Henry Louis Gates did a PBS show about my lineage in 2007. A lot of black folks in America had their history stolen and have no idea where their ancestors started out. What Dr. Gates uncovered in my case was that my great-great-grandparents became Florida homesteaders through the "forty acres and a mule" congressional act. These ancestors, William and Elise, showed up at the land office and didn't leave until they got forty acres and a mule for him and forty acres and a mule for her. Over one hundred thousand black people were emancipated after the Civil War, but only about six thousand became landowners like my great-great-grandparents. It was damn hard work. Dr. Gates told me he could understand how I got my feisty DNA. I found it fascinating, but my mother never wanted to hear about it or watch the show.

She was not at all interested in our family history, even the distant past, in any way. There was a reason for that. One that very few people knew.

Besides, nobody in the distant past or even the recent past was going to help her take care of herself or her two kids. She knew she had to be okay on her own.

Because of what happened to my mom when I was nine years old (coming up—I know you're going to look ahead, but come back here) and due to what she taught me as a kid, I learned how to be okay on my own, too. It framed my life.

But here's the thing that my mind won't wrap around. This is why my mom's death became the most devastating experience of my life: she really dug my brother and me. She was the most remarkable person I knew. A couple of days after she died, I realized that there would be no one on this earth who loved me as much as she did. I wouldn't put that kind of sparkle in anyone else's eye. She and my brother were my first loves.

I know she would be pissed off about me feeling this way and say, "Really? No one else loves you? Really. Come on. Get out of here."

Okay, I know I'm loved, and I've got those I love unconditionally. She's right. So, I got over myself. But I'll never get over her.

Chapter Three

In a black-and-white photo of me, one of the very few I have of myself as a little kid, I am sitting on the concrete steps of our apartment building. I'm about two years old. I'm bundled up in a full-body snowsuit; only there is no snow in the photo. I'm smiling, but my eyes are looking to the side, like, *What am I supposed to do here?* Somebody must have propped me up against the step because I'm so padded up, I don't know how I could move around on my own without help. But I had help. I had my older brother, Clyde.

When it snowed in New York in the '50s and '60s, it really snowed. It would come down for hours. It would pile up against the windows and freeze them shut. A good blizzard changed the look of the whole neighborhood. The playground equipment was buried. You couldn't tell where the edge of the sidewalk stopped and where the street began. There was no place for the plows to move the snow, so most of it stayed where it fell. The street traffic would stop altogether.

Those were the best times with my older brother. He'd carry his Flexible Flyer outside, and we'd sled down Tenth Avenue. He'd put me on the front of the sled and push the back end until it picked up some speed. Then Clyde would jump on. We'd laugh and holler, and I'd try not to tip over our ride by leaning too much.

There really aren't any hilly streets in Chelsea, you know, so it was all about momentum. We probably only slid half the block, but for a little kid, it could have been the Matterhorn. I would wear my brother out. As soon as the sled stopped moving, I'd say, "Again, Clyde. Do it again." He'd grab the rope, pull me back to the other end of the street, and repeat.

Sooner or later, all the kids in the surrounding buildings would tumble outdoors, and we'd stay for hours, having snowball fights and sledding until our faces were frozen.

It didn't matter who you were, or thought you were, when there was a good New York City blizzard. From Wall Street to the George Washington Bridge, everything came to a standstill. Nobody was going anywhere. It was the great equalizer.

The projects, at that time, were an ethnic enclave of a wide variety of folks: black, white, Chinese, Puerto Rican, Korean, Mexican, Italian, and Jewish. It was one big confusing jumble of languages and cultural traditions, but the kids adapted easily. We just rolled with it because that's all we knew. You didn't have to understand the words when a Puerto Rican mom scolded you in Spanish. The tone alone would dress you down. There were always five or six moms sitting on the benches surrounding the big playground between the buildings, ready to step in if you messed up. You didn't dare shove anybody or cut in ahead of your turn in double Dutch jump rope. Or you could look up at the buildings and see mom faces popping up here and there in the windows, checking on all the kids below. You couldn't get away with anything. By the time you rode the elevator to your own floor, your mom would already know what had happened and when.

On summer days, most of the kids would be sent outside after breakfast and told to come home when the sun went down. Instead of taking the time to go upstairs, the kids would call up to the open window of their apartment if they needed something.

When the Mister Softee or Good Humor ice cream truck would pull up next to the playground, I would shout up to the sixth-floor window of our apartment: "Ma! Ma! Can I have a quarter?"

She'd wrap a quarter in some tissues and drop it from the window into the hedges next to the building so it didn't smack anyone on the head and I could find it. Or sometimes I'd wait for the old guy with the Italian shaved ice cart. He'd wheel around a block of ice in a cooler and shave it off into a paper cone. Then he'd pour orange or cherry Kool-Aid over the top.

That was the only way we could cool off on summer days unless we got lucky and some teenage boys uncapped the fire hydrant. There was no air conditioning in any of the apartments. We didn't even have a fan. When it was a humid 95 degrees outside, it would feel like 115 degrees inside. The concrete-and-brick buildings would absorb the sun all day long and then be like radiators at night, pumping out the heat. We would run rags under the cold-water tap and wear them wrapped around our necks. That was our high-tech cooling system.

In the evenings, the buildings would peel open like a can of sardines, and people of all ages would bring down kitchen chairs and folding tables and set up outside, trying to catch any cool breeze possible. Old men would play dominoes and the young women would play cards, and I'd listen to them all talking and gossiping. Folks would stay outside as long as they could because trying to sleep in bed was impossible. You'd lie there all night long, flipping back and forth like a burger on a hot grill.

Whenever I could, I'd hang out with Clyde for the day. There's a big difference between ages six and twelve, but Clyde was such a cool cat that even his guy friends couldn't talk him out of having me go along.

They'd say, "You gotta take your sis with us?"

Clyde would answer, "I like taking Caryn. If you don't want to go, then that's okay. But I'm taking Caryn."

He took me everywhere. Before I was old enough to keep up with him, he'd make a skateboard by putting a two-by-four plank of wood between two skates. Then he'd wedge a box between the skates on the board. He'd put me in the box, push it along, and off we'd go. I learned a whole lot about how to be around boys and how they think.

I was Clyde's biggest fan. It didn't matter what he did. He was really good at softball. I'd stand off to the side and yell my head off when he was up to bat.

We'd ask our mom for some money before going outside.

She'd say, "Listen. If I had it, I'd give it to you. But

there's quite a bit of money right over in that corner."
She'd point over at the empty Coca-Cola and Hoffman
soda bottles. "If you gather those bottles and take them
back, you might get enough money to enable you to do
what you want."

We'd gather up the empties and take them back to
the store for the deposit return. Sometimes, if we were
lucky, it was enough to get a burger and fries at the Five
& Dime counter. Most often, it would only be enough
for penny candy. The jackpot was having an extra nickel
for a Bonomo Turkish Taffy. The tough part was pick-
ing between chocolate, banana, strawberry, or vanilla. I'd
carry it home, put the bar in the fridge, and get it really
cold before taking it out to the playground. The trick
was to put the cold taffy flat in your hand and smack
it down on the sidewalk. When I opened the package,
it would be broken up into about twelve pieces I could
share. The kid with the candy was always popular, at
least for a few minutes.

A couple of times during the summer, we'd get up
in the morning, and Ma would be making spiced-ham-
and-cheese sandwiches with Miracle Whip. Clyde and
I knew what that meant. We were going to Coney Island.
It was a big deal!

Ma loved Coney Island, and Clyde and I matched

her enthusiasm. She'd pack up a plastic cooler with the sandwiches, Wise potato chips, and maybe some peanut-butter-and-jelly sandwiches, too. Then she'd hand the cooler to Clyde, and we'd head to the Eighth Avenue train stop. The train would go underground for a while and then come up into the daylight, and we'd be in a different neighborhood, as if Brooklyn was a whole other country. At our stop we'd step off into a station that smelled of hot buttered popcorn, cotton candy, ocean air, and sweat. There was a long line of booths even before you left the station, selling all the carnival and beach things that were possible: balloons, beach balls and float rings, things that chirped and whirled, water pistols and yo-yos, and plastic Kewpie dolls tied to the ends of long bamboo sticks.

I really wanted one of those Kewpie dolls with a purple-and-pink feather dress and glitter glued on her head in the shape of a cap. I wanted to walk through Coney Island holding that cane up high like a victory flag.

My mother would stop me and say, "Look. We aren't buying that today. We're going to stick to where we are going and have a good time. You won't need a Kewpie. It won't be important anymore."

I'd say, "Okay. Okay." And she'd be right. We'd head out into Coney Island, and five minutes later I wouldn't think about the doll on a cane at all. At least until the next time we got off the train at Coney Island.

We'd spend the whole day going up and down the boardwalk, standing in lines for the Wild Mouse coaster, the Scrambler, and the centrifugal-force ride, a big tube that spins and then the floor drops out from under everybody. And you're laughing your ass off looking across at other folks just dangling on the wall.

Then there was the shop where you could buy a hand-dipped candy apple. They were making them there, right in front of you, swirling the apple on a stick in the hot red candy syrup, letting it cool a minute, and handing it to you on a cupcake paper. I'd have red candy stuck to every tooth in my mouth, but I didn't care.

We'd stop after a couple of hours and eat the lunch Ma had packed, saving the food money to get the best dinner: Nathan's hot dogs. Near the end of the day, we'd each get a hot dog in a paper boat and crinkle-cut french fries that came with a skinny wooden fork with two prongs. We'd sit there as the sun dropped down, eating our hot dogs and fries.

The sound of folks laughing, the clanging of the rides spinning or rolling, the merry-go-round music, the games, the smell of fried dough and cotton candy, hot dogs and fries. For me, it was heaven. My mom, brother, and I would spend the whole day at Coney Island, and I felt like we were untouchable, completely untouchable.

Another summer tradition was taking the Circle Line boats all around Manhattan, up the Hudson River, and out to Staten Island. We'd walk up the Statue of Liberty all the way to her crown, where you could stand and look down at the water and over at the Manhattan skyline. Mom would have us climb up all 354 steps every year, even when we complained. She'd say, "Come on. It's good for you."

It was good for me, even if I didn't know it at the time. From the top I could see the big picture of what humans were capable of making, all the skyscraper buildings, and the vast ocean surrounding our hometown city.

When I was a little older, Clyde and I would board a bus with most of the other kids in our neighborhood and go to Camp Madison-Felicia in Putnam Valley. The camp experience was provided by the Fresh Air Fund, which made it possible for city kids to get out into nature. Camp was days of activities: doing craft projects, roasting marshmallows, and eating hot dogs cooked on wire coat hangers over burning logs. We'd sing camp songs around the campfire every night, moving around to avoid whichever way the smoke was blowing. Camp was where I learned to swim in a lake, dive off a dock, and row a boat. We slept in wooden bunkhouses. I don't remember being worried about tick bites or having life jackets on in the rowboats. No one wore sunscreen, hats, or sunglasses. We even whittled pieces of wood with open jackknives, something they'd probably never let kids do now. It was all for fun. I don't think anybody had to go to the hospital.

As an adult, when folks heard where I grew up, they would act like I had survived a tough childhood. That's not my memory. I always thought as long as I had my mom and Clyde, that everything was going to be good. We watched out for each other.

I'm sure Clyde, being older, saw it all from a different perspective. He probably felt more responsibility being the male in the house. He never said that to me, but I did know there was always a special love between my mother and her firstborn, a place nobody else would hold. I mentioned that to my mom once, and she said, "It doesn't mean I don't love you. I love you both the best way I can."

I'd eventually see harsher realities as I got older, but it never came from her. Her whole day-to-day perspective was to live in the most practical manner possible. For my mom, that meant not letting other people's opinions take your attention or energy. She thought the most important opinion was what you thought of yourself and how you lived your life.

She held on to those standards her whole life. As I got older, I eventually understood the backbone that it took.

Chapter Four

I'm not much of a sleeper. I like the quiet of the night. Nothing is expected of you at three in the morning. You can do your own thing without being bothered by a phone call. There's no pressure to be social with anybody. I can get stuff done. Or do nothing at all.

Usually, I'm up and padding around the house with my cat, Twilight. We're both nocturnal. It's a lifelong pattern for both of us. It sometimes makes other people, who might be staying at my house, feel disturbed.

They'll say, "What are you doing? Why are you up? Go to bed."

They only ask me, never the cat.

I do rest. I lie down on the bed and listen to a good audiobook on my headphones. I might doze off for a couple of hours. Four hours is a lot of sleep for me.

When I was little, my mom used to send me to bed at a regular kid hour. She'd read to me, tuck me in, and kiss me goodnight. Then, she'd tiptoe back in to check on me an hour or two later. I'd still be wide-awake, looking out the window at the lights on in other windows or whatever part of the sky I could see. I'm sure it was frustrating for my mother.

She'd say, "Aren't you tired? Everybody needs sleep."

I didn't seem to need much sleep to be fine. I don't know why. It's just my make. My imagination is always busy. That has never changed. As a kid, I'd make up stories and give voices to inanimate objects in my room. Who could sleep when you've got your box of crayons having a conversation with your sneakers? You know, there's no reason to lie there lonely when you can bring inanimate objects to life. I still do it.

I don't know when my mother got to sleep either. When I started kindergarten, she worked at the French Hospital, which was this great hospital in Chelsea started by Catholic nuns. It closed down in the '70s.

She obtained her diploma from one of the only programs in the country that would educate black women who wanted to go into the nursing field. Her goal was to become a registered nurse, but that wasn't an option if you were black. So, she was a practical nurse in the

pediatric ward. She worked the overnight shift. It was
the best hours for her as a single mom with two children. There was no extra money for someone to watch
us if she worked daytime hours, so she'd trust us to go
to sleep while she worked nights. Clyde was in charge
at about age twelve. Off she'd go in her white nurse uniform, stockings, and white shoes. Black nurses weren't
allowed to wear their natural hair in the 1960s. She
would hot comb it until it was straight and then pin it
up under her nurse's cap. Most nights, she would leave
around 10:00 p.m. and be back at 6:30 or 7:00 a.m.,
in time to get Clyde and me up and ready for school.

When Clyde got into his teenage years, word got
around our neighborhood that our house was parent-free
overnight. We became the dance party place for all the teenagers. They would sneak out of their apartments around
midnight and show up at ours. The music would start up:
the Temptations, the Supremes, Smokey Robinson and
the Miracles, and James Brown. I learned all the dances
of that time from my brother and his friends at 2:00 a.m.

Sooner or later, one of them would notice me standing on the sidelines and say, "Go back to bed."

I'd try to stay. "Can I have some potato chips?"

"No! Get back in bed!"

Around four in the morning, everyone would start to

leave, and Clyde would throw away the trash and get in bed for a couple of hours of sleep before Mom got home.

I never ratted out my brother, but somebody did. I'm betting the folks in the apartments above, below, and next to us weren't happy with James Brown's "It's a Man's Man's Man's World" blasting after midnight from an apartment full of unsupervised teenagers. I'm sure Ma could tell stuff was going on long before the neighbor complained. When twenty people smoke in a small apartment with all the windows closed for four hours, it's going to stink. Teenagers are dumb.

Besides my mother keeping some reins on a growing teenage boy, there was me, pulling the midnight special. If my mother was able to grab a couple hours of sleep in the morning, that might have been it. At my Catholic elementary school, we'd be sent home for lunch every day, so I don't think she slept much.

I was not only a nonsleeper; I was a noneater. I had a big wide range of taste when it came to candy, except for black licorice (who the fuck thought that was a treat?), and a limited palate when it came to real food. I would eat my Cheerios dry in the morning. I liked to keep it simple. I still do. I don't like anything globby, mushy, wet, or hidden under a sauce or gravy.

Eggs, no matter how you cook them, fit into too

many of those descriptions. From the second the shell was cracked on the edge of the frying pan, I left the room. That clear, gooey gel and yellow slimy yolk were never going to turn into something I'd eat. I gagged at the smell of eggs cooking.

One day, my mother decided to broaden my food horizons. I was in second grade, and I came to the table for breakfast dressed in my plaid Catholic girl uniform and a white blouse, ready for school. On my plate were scrambled eggs.

I looked at my mom like she was joking with me. She wasn't.

She said, "Caryn, you can't decide you don't like something if you never try it."

Yeah, that is probably practical and reasonable, especially since Clyde would eat anything and everything she put on his plate.

I didn't talk back about it, though. I thought she'd understand my point of view if I held out. So, I sat there, not trying the eggs.

I didn't get anything else for breakfast, and after about twenty minutes, I got sent out the door for school.

I wasn't going for a standoff, but I was sure she now understood that eggs were not something I was ever going to eat. It looked like Ma had decided to push the matter some more because when I came home for lunch, those scrambled eggs were still on the table, waiting for me.

I couldn't believe it. At some point she let me know I wouldn't get anything else to eat until I, at the very least, tried a bite of eggs.

"It's important for you to try new things," she told me, not unkindly but firmly. "It's good for you."

If I could have, I would have, just to make her happy. But that shit now looked like cold pig slop. It wasn't leaving the plate on my fork. I didn't care. I wasn't giving in. I waited until time was up and headed back to school.

Like in a horror movie, right when you think that monster has to be dead for good, those eggs had survived and were still there on my plate after school. They even looked bigger, like they had multiplied. My mom had probably made fresh ones to prevent botulism. There wasn't a snack in sight. I didn't know how much longer she was going to hold out on giving me some real food, but I was going to hold out longer. I wasn't going to eat eggs at age seven, twenty-seven, or forty-seven. I still haven't had an egg at age sixty-seven.

No other food was offered, but I was okay because I had a small stash of candy in my room. Hey, what kid wouldn't rather eat candy for supper?

The next morning, nothing was said, but life was

back to normal: dry Cheerios and a cup of orange juice.

I learned a great lesson from my mom on this one, especially useful when I became a mom myself. Sometimes you've got to let the kid have their way. You've got to believe they know what they're talking about. If they can't stand to do something and no incentive changes their mind, then you have to back down.

My mom was smart enough to see that my eating eggs was never going to happen.

As I got a little older, she tried a variety of tactics to get me to eat different foods. If there was a plate of food before me that didn't fit my simple tastes, she'd say, "You better eat that food or I might have to send it to children in Ethiopia who would be happy to have it because they're hungry."

After age eight, I knew that would never happen. I didn't say anything out loud, but I'd be thinking, *How are you going to send this? In a Tupperware? Is there a place you go to drop it off to be sent to Ethiopia? How long would it take to get there?*

Years and years later, she was at one of my shows on Broadway, and I told the story of her saying that I wouldn't survive a disaster because I was such a picky eater. So, I pointed her out to the audience. "Yeah, sitting right here in the front is my mom."

Then, I said to her, "Do you realize that had there been a nuclear thing that happened in the '60s, it would have been you and Clyde who would have had a hard time? I'd get by okay since I didn't have to eat."

She was laughing so hard the tears were running down her face. And when I saw her after the show, she asked me, "How long did it take you to figure that out?"

She really did try her best to get me to eat better. I'm sure she would have liked me to be more adventurous in the food department, but that didn't happen. Not then. Not now. She got herself a quirky kid in almost every category.

My mother was into expanding her mind and showing us a larger world in any way possible. Education was a very big deal. Since childhood, she had been curious about many different things and loved learning. She was interested in ancient history, music, literature, art, and creative writing.

We had the Will and Ariel Durant book series The Story of Civilization in our house, and every couple of months, a new Time-Life book would arrive. If I asked her why something was the way it was in a movie we watched, she would say, "There's a book right over there on the shelf that will give you more information about what really happened."

Anything that I might be interested in, she would

take the time to encourage me, saying, "You can parlay the little bit that you know about a subject into something much more."

Whatever she wanted to know, she'd get books in the library and read up on it. Sometimes, the three of us would go to the huge New York Public Library on Forty-Second Street and Fifth Avenue, across from Bryant Park. We'd walk the hallways and stop in the various rooms, especially the Rose Reading Room, with its clouds painted on the ceiling forty-five feet above our heads. I'm sure if my mom didn't have us kids to look after, a lot of her days off would have been spent right there in the Rose Room, surrounded by fifty thousand books.

She could discuss a wide variety of subjects. And she was funny. She would have fit right in at the Algonquin Round Table lunches that took place in the 1920s, where writers like Robert Benchley, Dorothy Parker, and George S. Kaufman would get together every day and shoot the shit about any subject that came up. She would sit and write when she could, but she'd put it all away.

Later on in my life, I thought of my mother as an undiscovered George Sand, the female novelist from the 1800s who published under a man's name to be allowed to write what she wanted. My mother had a brilliant mind but did not have the opportunity to express her potential. I know, later in her life, she submitted a few things to magazines. As she told me, "I've got many envelopes that hold rejections."

Many women who lived in our housing division would react rather distant and cool toward my mother. They saw her interest in opera, art, and Roman history as unrelatable. And my mom was unwilling to speak badly about other people, so she didn't join in on the gossip benches outside. They couldn't figure out why her husband was gone, and they were a little suspicious that she might steal away theirs.

My mom just blew it off. She would say, "I got two kids of my own. Why would I want her man and four more of his kids?"

In the 1960s, the New York art scene was busting out with modern and pop art. It was radical in its definition and pushed the limits of what people considered art. We'd go to MoMA to see what it was all about. There was Andy Warhol's tomato soup can and Roy Lichtenstein's graphic art that I dug, being a big comic book fan. We each had our favorite artists. Mine was Maxfield Parrish. Still is.

Every year, Ma would take us to the Ice Capades, which I loved, when it came to Madison Square Garden. The costumes were phenomenal, and they would slide giant set pieces out onto the ice. We'd also go see the Ringling Bros. and Barnum & Bailey Circus when it toured in New York.

I knew I couldn't ask Ma for too much stuff from the vendors going up and down the aisles hawking cotton candy and peanuts in the shell, but she would almost always get me a souvenir program book that I would look at over and over at night when I wasn't sleeping.

Since I was already up all night, giving voices to a box of crayons, headphones, jump ropes, and sneakers, Mom thought I'd dig a good puppet show. There was a couple, Bil and Cora Baird, who created puppets and marionettes and had their own theater space in the Village. I was enthralled by it all. Every couple of months, they would put on a new show, and my mother would make sure we went together. It helped me feel a little less weird, seeing these two adult people who had a whole career in making wooden things move and talk.

She also found a way for the three of us to go to Radio City Music Hall and see every Rockettes show. In the 1960s the Rockettes would do their show, and then the curtains would part and there would be a giant CinemaScope movie screen. She took us to see *How the West Was Won*, one of the first movies shot in Cinerama style. I'm sure that's where we saw *The Sound of Music* (which featured Bil and Cora Baird's marionettes in "The

Lonely Goatherd" when the kids and Maria put on a show for their father and the countess). We also went to see *Camelot* when it first came out.

I would sit there before the movie and imagine myself becoming a Rockette one day. Somehow, it seemed possible, even though there wasn't one dancer in that whole line of thirty-six women who looked anything like me. They all matched each other, but none of them looked like me. (It was 1987 before a black child saw a Rockette that looked like her. The organization has been scrambling to fix it all in the last couple decades, which is good. Every kid should see a skin color close to their own in that lineup.)

Our favorite time to see the Rockettes was always the Christmas Spectacular. My mother turned our lives into a Christmas Spectacular at home, too. Like everything else she made happen, it was all very mysterious to me. She could make stuff appear out of thin air.

It would start when Macy's in Herald Square, the flagship store on Thirty-Fourth Street, decorated their windows for the holidays. Every window would have a theme or a story to it. We'd walk around the entire building and then head over to Gimbels department store a block away to see if their Christmas windows could match up with Macy's.

About five days later, we'd get up for school, and

there would be a fresh-cut evergreen tree in a red metal stand set up in the living room. I knew it was there before I saw it because the pine smell would travel down the hall. We had no clue how our mom could get that tree in the house and up on the stand, but if I asked her, she'd look at me seriously and say, "How do you think it got here?"

The next thing that would happen is, one morning, we'd come out to breakfast, and the windows would be covered with spray-snow stencils of Santa, elves, Rudolph, a sleigh, snowmen, and Christmas trees.

On the last day of school before Christmas week, we'd come home and see the boxes of Christmas decorations, strings of lights, and ornaments next to the tree. Our apartment was very small, so I never knew where the boxes were kept the rest of the year.

I'd ask my mom about that, too, and she'd answer, "I have no idea what you're asking me. They came from wherever they were."

My mother was determined to keep the season as magical as possible for us kids.

That night, the three of us would play Bing Crosby and Nat King Cole Christmas albums and decorate the tree. We'd laugh and dance around, tossing handfuls of silver tinsel as high on the tree as we could. Then, Mom would plug in the red, green, yellow, and orange string of lights, and we'd turn off all the other lights in the house and take in our tree design.

Every day after that, I'd look to see if there were any presents under the tree, but there never were. If my mother wasn't home, I'd search the house with a fine-tooth comb trying to find hidden gifts. Nothing. The only wrapped item under the tree before Christmas Day would be whatever Clyde and I bought for Ma. We'd have scraped together a month or two of Hoffman bottle returns and gotten her some Jean Nate bath powder or a necklace. We'd wrap up crafts we had made through a city park program. She'd always act like it was something she really wanted.

On the night before Christmas, I remember Walter Cronkite would sign off the evening news by saying something like, "Right now there is no war or fighting going on anywhere, and there is peace all around the world. We wish you a very happy holiday." And that was when I felt like we would all be okay—for the next couple days, everybody would be safe. Then, we'd turn the TV to the local channel (WPIX) that aired the continuous burning of a Yule log in a fireplace and played Christmas music.

At 8:00 p.m., Ma would take the thawed Butterball turkey out of the fridge and get it ready to bake. She'd pull out the bag of giblets and rinse out the cavity. (I should have paid better attention because as an adult I left that bag in the hole once. Big mistake.) She'd arrange the turkey on a stand so she could stuff it up with Pepperidge Farm traditional stuffing that she had seasoned. Before the stuffing went in, she put a cut-up stick of butter inside and then the mixed-up stuffing on top of it. Once the turkey was in the pan, we perforated the outside with a knife to make entry points for all of the basting sauce, which was about ten sticks of sliced butter, a cup of water, salt and pepper, and whatever dripped from the cooking turkey.

At 9:00 p.m. she'd put the turkey in the oven at 270 degrees and then baste it every hour, probably all night long.

I'd have my mind set on staying up to watch *A Christmas Carol*, starring Alastair Sim, the original British version, which usually came on at 11:30 p.m. Clyde and I would sit there with bags under our eyes and our lids propped open. I'd give it my full effort to make it to Tiny Tim's "God bless us, everyone," but would usually nod out around when the Ghost of Christmas Future made his appearance. Clyde would shuffle me off to bed. At some time in the middle of the night, Clyde would shake my shoulder and whisper, "Come out with me to the living room."

We'd tiptoe out of my room and look into the living room. We couldn't get close because our mom would be sleeping on the couch. The tree would be twinkling in the dark, and under and next to it would be a sea of wrapped presents. Some, like new bikes, would just have bows on them. One Christmas, a Lionel train set was running around the tree. It would be the best sight in the world, and I would be blown away that it had all happened while I was sleeping for a couple hours. We'd have to go back to bed because Ma wasn't going to let us open presents until after breakfast.

The next morning we'd float out of our rooms on the aroma of roasting turkey and stuffing and fresh pine Christmas tree. We'd unwrap gifts for hours. There would be games like Parcheesi and Sorry!, a Flintstones magic movie projector, which I'd lose my mind over, a Chatty Cathy doll, and Tressy, whose hair grew to her waist by pushing a button on her stomach. My favorite present one year was a Frosty snow-cone machine, where you would put ice cubes in his hat and rotate the handle on the back to make your own snow cones. It came with paper cone cups and squeeze bottles of flavoring. There were new snow boots and a new dress, which didn't thrill me, but one disliked gift in fifteen isn't bad.

Later in the day, the three of us would stuff ourselves

with turkey, rice, and stuffing. I left all the greens and cranberry sauce to Clyde and Ma. All I wanted was for the three of us to be together, and that's what made it Christmas.

The decorated tree would stay up until we went back to school in January. Then, one day we'd get home after school, and it would all be gone, like it had magically disappeared. I'd be even more determined to find out where the boxes of decorations were kept in our apartment, but it never happened. I couldn't even uncover a leftover strand of tinsel, no matter how long I looked.

The mystery of how my mother made all of this happen remains unsolved. Even as an adult, she never told me how she got us all those gifts. I imagine she started putting stuff on layaway in February. And I never did figure out where she kept them all hidden until midnight on Christmas Eve or where all the decorations went in January.

One time when I was an adult, Mom, Clyde, and I were talking about the upcoming Christmas. I knew I couldn't ask Ma anything outright. So, I tried to circle around the question.

"I was just thinking about when we were kids. Where did you put everything, you know, all the decorations and presents at Christmas?"

She looked over at Clyde, then back at me, as if I were speaking a different language. "What are you talking about? I have no idea what it is you're asking me."

I started to feel dopey, thinking, *Really? Am I not asking it correctly?*

"Ma, the apartment was so small. And there was a lot of stuff. Where was it all?"

She answered, "Well, where do you think it all came from?"

To this day, I have no idea how she did it. Her attitude was firm. "Why do you need to know that? Why can't I tell you Santa Claus brought it? Why isn't that enough?"

She never spilled her secrets. She'd just smile, look at me sideways, and say, "It's all magical as far as I know."

Whatever it was, I still keep Ma's traditions going. Every December I have to put up a fresh-cut evergreen tree and slow-roast a turkey overnight to feel like it is Christmas.

I don't even mind being the person who bastes the turkey every hour all night long because, you know, I'm not a big sleeper.

Chapter Five

Going to Queens, on its own, would have been like a new adventure, but the three of us, Ma, Clyde, and I, had a destination. And it was huge—the 1964 World's Fair. There were pavilions for miles in all different styles of architecture that represented other countries. There were food booths and restaurants with things I had never seen people eat. There were hundreds of exhibits that blew the three of us away. We walked by massive dinosaur sculptures in Dinoland and the big Unisphere ball that represented the globe; the "It's a Small World" ride was there; and a skyway tram took us from one end of the fair to the other so we could look down on the thousands of folks below.

The Bell Telephone Company pavilion had prototypes of the Picturephone (think big-screen FaceTime, but forty-six years before it was available to the public). You could dial up and talk to somebody in a completely different area and see their face. It was like magic. As an up-and-coming sci-fi fan, I also loved Futurama II. It was supposed to represent life in the US in the year 2064, with space folks zooming around wearing jet packs. I guess my great-grandkids will get to see how that all turns out.

It's a good thing we can't see into the future. Even as a kid, I had no idea how drastically my future and my whole personal world would change in the next couple of years.

One afternoon I came home from elementary school and found my mother standing in the hallway, looking in the coat closet. Her hair was completely disheveled, sticking out all over her head. Without even seeing her face, I knew something was really wrong. She would have never let her hair look like that. She was barefoot and wearing a black trench coat open over a white slip. She was muttering incoherently to herself and didn't even seem to notice I was home. Then she turned around and looked toward the bedrooms. I didn't know what to do. Clyde wasn't home, and I knew I couldn't leave her like this. I watched as she went over to the oven, turned it on, opened the door, and put her head in there.

I was old enough to know this was really bad news. I ran over and grabbed her around the waist and pulled her out.

"Ma! Mommy, what are you doing?"

She stayed there, kneeling on the floor, mumbling something. I reached up and turned the oven off.

"Mommy, are you okay?"

Then, she said clearly, "Go get Miss Viola."

Miss Viola was a neighbor my mother liked who lived one floor below us.

I ran down the stairwell and knocked on her door. She seemed annoyed to have her day interrupted. I was having a hard time formulating words to ask her for help. I didn't know how to explain what was happening. I stood at her door, motioning for her to come with me.

"What's the matter? What's going on?" She asked me about three times.

Finally, I got out the words, "Something's wrong with Mommy."

Miss Viola followed me up the stairwell and into our apartment. I stood by the hall closet and watched as she bent over my mother. Ma mumbled something incoherent. I watched as Miss Viola spoke to Ma and then helped her get up and sit in a chair. She went to the wall phone and made a call.

The paramedics arrived with a gurney. They were moving my mother from her chair when Clyde got home from school. He became frantic.

"What's going on? What's happening to Ma?"

I told him, "I don't know. I found her like this. Don't get mad at me."

Then Clyde started freaking out and got puffed up with the paramedics, trying to get them away from our mom.

"Don't touch her. Wait! Leave her be."

They weren't about to listen to a kid, though, and Ma didn't seem to notice Clyde either.

When they wheeled her onto the elevator, I got on it, too. Other people were already on the elevator, and I felt protective and pissed off. I was thinking, *Don't look at my mother. Mind your own business.*

But that wasn't going to happen in our building. By the time they wheeled her out the front door and loaded her in the ambulance, all the neighbors were looking down from windows on every floor.

I tried to climb into the ambulance next to my mom, but the driver stopped me.

"I want to go with her. Let me go with her."

Miss Viola pulled me back. "You can't go. Kids can't go in hospitals."

By this time, Clyde had come down the stairs and was standing on the sidewalk next to me as the ambulance turned on the siren and drove off with our mother inside.

I didn't know what to do next. *Do we go back upstairs? What is going to happen?*

Clyde took my shoulder and steered me to the front door. "Come on. Let's go."

We rode the elevator back up to our floor and went inside. I stood in the middle of the room, not grasping what was happening.

"Clyde, what are we supposed to do now?"

I remember Clyde made some phone calls to our father and our grandfather, Ma's dad.

"It'll be all right. It will be fine," Clyde told me. I could tell by his voice that he didn't really believe it.

It wasn't fine. It was the last time I saw my mother for two whole years.

No one explained to me what had happened. I only knew that she was in the hospital and kids weren't allowed to go.

I didn't understand until later that my mother had been sent to Bellevue Hospital for having a nervous breakdown.

She had been acting differently for a couple of

months, like she wanted to be alone and not have me and Clyde to think about. One night, I woke up to see my mother standing over me, staring at me without saying anything. I asked her what was going on. She didn't answer. She only walked out of the room. Years later, Clyde told me he had found her with a pair of scissors, acting strangely. He had taken the scissors from her.

I had also been noticing that her head would shake from side to side when she talked to me. I had asked her, "Why does your head keep shaking?"

She'd dismiss me and say, "It's not shaking."

I left it alone.

She never talked about her feelings. She kept it all contained with a self-sufficient attitude. If any adults saw my mom's nervous breakdown coming, I never knew it. She'd never say if she was lonely or hurt. She didn't show if she was worried. That was how it was for her generation. Folks didn't talk about their feelings. The word *stress* didn't even exist in everyday language. It was part of life, everyone trying to get by. I guess they thought vulnerable types of feelings should be private stuff . . . even between family members.

Ma solved her problems on her own because she had to. She didn't have any help, and she was never comfortable asking anyone for a favor. The one time she asked for a little assistance from my dad's mother, my grand-mother, she was treated unkindly. There were no child support laws in the 1960s. Women couldn't get a bank loan without a husband to cosign or even a credit card with just her name on it.

Having my mom taken away and hospitalized was like having a Band-Aid ripped off and facing the real world all of a sudden. I have very few memories of those two years without my mother being there, and maybe that was because no one would talk to me about it or tell me what was going on. I kind of remember my mom's cousin Arlene staying with us, some other cous-ins coming and going for a while, and our father being there off and on. But I couldn't get from them what I'd always had with my mom. I had a key, and I'd let myself in after school and wait for Clyde to come home. I have no idea how the rent got paid, what we ate for meals, how I had clean clothes to wear, or any other everyday living thing. It all happened somehow, but I don't know how or when. None of the holidays without my mom are in my memory. I don't recall being at school and going on to the next grade, but I know I did. No one asked me about it. Nobody told me it would be okay or that I'd see my mom again. I only had the same thought, every single day: *Don't ask anyone for anything. Be good. Don't cause any trouble. Stay to yourself. As long as your brother is here, you'll be okay.*

I felt that I'd have to be self-sufficient and that being kept from my mom by the adults was bullshit. I held back from telling any of them anything. It's not like I was going to discuss how my day was at school with my dad, who never seemed to care anyway. I knew Clyde and I would be better off without any of them there. But I didn't have a choice. It's probably classic trauma stuff for kids who don't feel safe, but I learned by necessity that I had to count on myself and hoped that nothing would happen to my brother. I knew he'd never let anything happen to me, and I'd never let anything happen to him if I could stop it.

A couple of times during those two years, I'd ask Clyde, "Do you think Ma is ever going to come back?"

He'd say, "Yeah, sure. Why wouldn't she? We're her kids."

"Yeah, yeah. You're right. We're her kids. She's going to come back."

I tried to go with it, to believe Clyde had the answer. He may have known more of what was happening with our mother, but I doubt it. He never told me if he did.

I spent some of my after-school hours and Saturday mornings watching cartoons. My mom used to love to

watch them all, too, as they'd show the older classics fea-
turing characters like Felix the Cat, Koko the Clown, and
Betty Boop with Minnie the Moocher. I'd watch Rocky
and Bullwinkle, Huckleberry Hound, Mighty Mouse,
Popeye, the Flintstones, all the Bugs Bunny and Road
Runner cartoons.

I'd collect comic books and get new ones if given a
little change, reading about Archie and Jughead, Nancy
and Sluggo, Richie Rich, Tom and Jerry, Wendy the
Good Little Witch, or Casper the Friendly Ghost.

Then, one day, when we got home from school,
our father and grandfather met us at the door. And our
grandfather said, "Look, your mom is back home."

Clyde and I ran in to see her, shouting, "Ma! Ma!"

She hugged us both, but she looked like she wasn't
sure what was going on.

I thought maybe she didn't like being hugged on
much because she had been in the hospital for so long.
But she didn't respond to hugs at all, even weeks later.
She would look at me like she was trying to figure out
what I wanted and what she was supposed to do for me
and Clyde.

The best way to describe the difference in her is
like in the 1956 sci-fi horror movie *Invasion of the Body
Snatchers*, where the young woman says something like,

"He looks and sounds like Uncle Ira, but it's not him." This woman in our living room looked like my mom and sounded like my mom. But it wasn't her.

I had no one to tell that to. I tried to say it to Clyde. I could see it bothered him, too.

He answered me, "Well, you know, it's Ma. Leave it alone."

Then I said, "She's different."

He said, "Well, she's been in the hospital."

She never left the apartment on her own. She would stay home until Clyde and I got back from school.

Every few days Clyde would ask her, "When are we going shopping? Should we go soon?"

The things our mother would always do on her own became a group effort, but that was okay with me. I loved going to supermarkets and looking at everything. The market nearest us was Daitch Shopwell, and it had all these amazing older women working there, wearing hairnets and running the registers with cigarettes hanging out of their mouths. They could ring up anything without looking at the price sticker because they had them memorized from working there for so long.

They would wave and smile at Ma, and she would wave back, but she didn't seem to know who they were or why they were waving hello.

We'd make our way up and down the aisles, getting what we needed and sometimes stuff we didn't need. Clyde and I would side-eye each other and grin because Ma was now okay with us getting snacks she had never agreed to before. We loved Cheez Doodles and Yodels (a chocolate-covered roll-up cake). She wanted them, too.

Mom would get vegetables and steam them for dinner. We didn't eat much meat, but sometimes we'd walk her over to the fish market on Ninth Avenue, which my friend Kathleen DiMartino's family owned, and get fish for dinner.

Little by little, she knit back together the routine stuff that was part of her life before hospitalization. After going somewhere a few times with me and Clyde, she would remember that she could go to Dan Bell's on the corner, and they would give credit if she needed it. She figured out where to go to buy her cigarettes.

As much as I couldn't wait for her to be back home with us, things were different. She didn't return to work at the French Hospital. It took a long time for her to be confident enough to go out on her own, and no adult explained why to me or Clyde. They all acted like things were back to the way they used to be. They also never made me or Clyde think that our mom had a nervous breakdown because of the two of us. So Clyde and

I didn't have to go through any guilt about what had happened to her.

We didn't know, at that time, why she was so different, but we chalked it up to thinking that people must get kind of standoffish if they've been hospitalized for a long time. Maybe they get tired of folks being up in their face. It made me question if I even really remembered who she used to be. Maybe she had never been a huggy type before, and I only thought she had been.

When I was a little kid, I understood that you had to be a certain size and age to lay up on somebody. But after that age, like around seven, you didn't do the physical stuff. Adults would expect you to be more self-contained and not need to touch and hug that much. I liked hugging as a kid and still wanted to hug my mother even as an older kid.

But after her hospitalization, her drama was such that I would say, "Can I hug you?"

And she'd say, "No. Not right now."

I'd say, "Okay," but then when I went to walk away, she'd call my name. So I'd stop.

Then she'd say, "Come here." And she would hug me. She'd say, "Okay, that's it. Okay?" And she let me go.

Those hugs were just for me. She never went back to being a hugger.

About forty years later, I finally found out what was really going on for her.

One afternoon, my mother, brother, and I were talking at my house in Berkeley, California.

I don't know what led up to me saying this, but I told her, "You know, Ma, when you went away for those two years, I think it was the best thing that could have happened to me. I know it was unhappy for you, but it changed everything for me."

She said, "Really?"

"Oh, yeah. It made me see things differently. It really drove home to me that I had to do stuff on my own. I had to figure things out."

"Like what?"

"I had to figure out who I was going to be."

She said, "Can I tell you something?"

I was like, "Sure. Of course."

Mom looked at Clyde and then at me. "I didn't know who you were. When I got home from the hospital."

My brother and I both said the same thing: "What? What do you mean? Of course you knew who we were."

Then she went on to tell this story that stunned my brother and me. Afterward, it all seemed to make perfect sense to us in a way that we hadn't contemplated before.

In the same way a woman couldn't get a bank loan or

a credit card on her own in the 1960s, she also couldn't decide on her own health care. Because she was still married to my father, he and my grandfather got to decide what happened to her after she was taken by the ambulance. These two men, who were barely ever around my mom, approved of her having experimental electroshock therapy.

As she talked, I sat there feeling awful for her that she had been sent to a mental hospital and had to stay for two years. After all, it might have all been prevented if they had helped her out along the way. All she wanted to do was get some help. And nobody would help her. Nobody.

Then, after God knows how many electroshock therapy treatments and who the fuck knows what else they tried out on her, they decided she was no longer crazy. One day the doctor came to her bed and said, "Okay. It's over. You're getting out. You're going home."

She had no idea what that meant following so many brain-altering treatments. But she wasn't going to say, "What do you mean? I'm going home? Where is that?"

They expected she would know she had two children and where she lived. But the truth was she had no memory of her previous life. All she wanted was for them to get away from her so they couldn't see that she was unsure and then change their minds.

Her father and husband, who were like two strangers, took her to our apartment in Chelsea, and in came these two kids she didn't recognize.

Sitting at my kitchen table, she told Clyde and me that she remembered thinking, *I have no idea who any of these people are, but I am never going back to that hospital again. No matter what. So whatever they say to me is what I'll accept.*

Clyde and I both sat there listening, speechless about what our mother was telling us all these decades later. But it all made sense.

Little by little, my mother had to solve the mystery of who she used to be and what her life had been like before Bellevue. And she had to do it without anyone knowing she didn't remember much at all. Some of her memory came back on its own after time, and some things were a complete start-over for her. But as soon as she was free, she made a choice that lasted her whole life. She would never work in a hospital, be taken to a hospital, see a doctor, or even a dentist ever again. She was never going to allow anyone to make a decision regarding her future care. She didn't want to give anybody the chance to decide she was crazy or sick. It had been taken out of her hands once, and she was never going to put herself in a position where that could possibly happen again.

Later in her life, Clyde and I would suggest that she should see a health professional for various reasons. She refused to go. Even when she was losing some of her teeth, she wouldn't let me get her a dentist appointment.

She'd say, "I'm okay with losing a couple teeth. I'm not going."

After she died, the doctor told us that the aneurysm wasn't her first brain issue, that she had probably had a number of small strokes before the fatal one.

That made sense too. I had been doing a FaceTime call with her a couple weeks before, and her face on one side looked swollen or stiff. I asked her about it. She said she had a bad tooth. I suggested the dentist, and once again, she refused.

In retrospect, I'm sure it was a stroke. But I didn't get it then.

Clyde suffered terrible guilt after the doctor told us about the multiple strokes. He said he should have noticed.

I told him, "Clyde, you wouldn't have noticed. If Ma didn't want to be seen, she wouldn't let you see her. She had her TV, books, a phone, and cigarettes in her room, and she wouldn't come out when she didn't want to deal with anyone."

If she had told Clyde and me that she was having

strokes, we probably would have fucked it up and forced her into a hospital or something she never wanted to do. She knew it, too. So she kept it to herself.

Clyde still felt bad, like he could have done something to prevent her from dying. But the truth is she brought us up to make our own choices. She made hers.

About ten years before she died, the three of us were talking about all the crazy shit that was going on in nursing homes when CBS started tracking abuse cases happening there.

My mother said, "Don't ever do that to me."

"Do what, Ma?"

"Put me in a nursing home."

"Why would I ever do that?" I asked her.

She said, "You might not be able to take care of me here."

Later, I asked Clyde why Ma was feeling worried about it.

He told me, "She's been watching and reading about all these terrible things happening to older folks in the nursing homes."

"But I would never send her there," I said.

"Listen, Caryn. There is no guarantee that we are going to have the money or that you will always be who you currently are in your career," Clyde said.

I thought about it. It made sense. She had been sent

away before, against her will. She wanted us to know she never wanted that to happen again.

For that reason, it's a good thing she went quickly. I thought to myself, *Thank you, God, that I don't ever have to consider who would take care of her and where.* I never had to make that kind of decision. Lots of people do have to make those choices for their parents or a sibling. Clyde died very fast, like that, in the same way. I wasn't ready for him to go, but I was still grateful I didn't have to make any choices for him either.

Chapter Six

My mother always knew I would be in the spotlight one day. As she told it, the moment I was born, I opened my eyes wide, checked out the people looking at me, and instantly turned my face toward the light. It's unusual for a newborn to arrive with open eyes and to keep them open. It was so rare that the delivery doctor and nurses summoned other medical staff to come into the birthing room and see this baby with a bunch of attitude.

I liked hearing that as a kid. Of course, I don't remember the actual event, but it seems I came up with a mission statement while floating around in the amniotic fluid. From the time my memory kicked in around age three or four, I knew I wanted to act.

Before I ever stepped on any actual stage, I had some "acting" training I did myself. I had to convince the

teaching nuns at St. Columba, my Catholic elementary
school, that I could read. Reading seemed to come easy
to other kids in my class, but when I looked at the words
on the page, the letters were all flipped around and jittery
and didn't make sense. They didn't stay in an order my
brain could process. So, I memorized what other kids in
my class read out loud. I locked it in my brain and then
acted like I was reading it off the page. Because my last
name was Johnson, there were at least six or seven kids
ahead of me in the alphabet who read out loud before
my turn, which gave me time to memorize what I was
supposed to be reading.

Nobody in the 1960s was talking about dyslexia.
I never even knew there was a diagnosis for what my
brain did to the alphabet. I only knew I had to make it
look like I didn't have a problem.

At first, my mom, who loved books and read when-
ever she could, was unconvinced. When I told her
I wasn't exactly figuring out this reading thing, she said,
"Well, do your best."

After a while, she realized that I really was trying
hard and that I was telling her the truth. I had no idea
how the other kids were reading the mess I saw in our
schoolbooks. My mom never made me feel bad about it.
She would simply tell me that I learned differently from

other children and that was okay. At night, she would read to me before bed, and I'd learn through listening. She'd read *Grimms' Fairy Tales* or other classic stories.

Years later, I would hear from other people with dyslexia how they were told they were lazy or not smart or made to feel like something was really wrong with them. My mother did the opposite. She always encouraged me to search for ways to learn and to look into anything I found interesting. She never told me that I was limited in any way.

She would remind me, "Listen, you can do anything you want to do. It's going to take you a little bit longer. You'll have to figure a couple of things out. But you can do that."

Top on her list was that she wanted me to figure out if I was going to be okay with being an individual, no matter what.

"You know, there's nothing wrong with going with the pack," she would tell me. "But if you insist on being an individual, it could possibly be a lot harder for you. Not everybody's going to get who you are. They're not all going to even want it around. And some folks won't want you to do what you want to do. But, if you're okay with that, then you'll be fine. That's all that matters."

When I was little, there were acting companies like

Joseph Papp's ensemble that did street theater. They would pull up to the curb along the avenue in a box truck that carried the stage set, and then a VW van would arrive with the actors. They'd set up the stage and some chairs for people to sit in, get into their costumes and makeup, and put on shows for the neighborhood. It was usually an expanded scene or a one-act play with kid-friendly content. I would be captivated by these shows and couldn't wait until I saw that box truck pull into place on the street for another one.

The Hudson Guild had a theater space nearby in a community center and did productions by adults and some children's theater. My mom encouraged me to go audition. Being able to play a character, to become someone or something else, was what I loved doing most. I was hooked.

My mom understood my honest struggle with school, but she was not at all impressed by another early-on acting job I tried to pull off. The Hudson Guild was sometimes given free tickets to various performances around town to share with students or people involved in theater production. One November, they gave some of us tickets to see *The Nutcracker* at Lincoln Center. I was about eleven, which was old enough to take the bus on my own.

That morning my mother told me, "Listen. Make sure you clean your room before you leave for *The Nutcracker*."

My room was a mess. I had stuff out everywhere. It never bothered me. I'd only grudgingly clean it because she constantly reminded me to get it picked up.

I told her, "Okay, Ma."

She went out to do whatever she had scheduled to do that day. I knew it was something that would last for five or six hours.

Suddenly, I felt like I had a split personality: a good Caryn and a bad Caryn, one sitting on my right shoulder, the other on my left.

The good Caryn, who always did the right thing, reminded me, "Let's get going and clean the room up."

Then a really convincing bad Caryn popped up on my left shoulder, saying, "Fuck that. You'll be back an hour before she comes home. You can do it then. Forget her. Go catch the bus."

The bad Caryn gave the ol' one-two to the good Caryn, knocking her off the right shoulder, and I pulled on my jacket, locked the door, and headed down the stairs.

The performance was great, and I floated home with the bad Caryn grinning and saying, "See? I told you we'd have time before your mother got home."

I was triumphant about my choice until I reached into my jacket pocket for the house key. It was gone. I checked every pocket. Nothing. I tried to figure out why the door was locked if I never took my key. I must have locked it. The key must have fallen out. I didn't have time to get back to Lincoln Center to see if it was under my seat. My heart started to race.

My brother was not around anywhere, and I didn't know where to find him. The office of the housing authority was shut up for the day.

The clock was running out, and my mind was saying over and over, "I don't know what to do. I don't know what to do."

I was standing in the hallway with no way to get inside. I thought maybe if I could climb out of the window at the end of the hall and crawl across window ledges over to our apartment at the front of the building, I could push our window open and get in. As I looked out the hallway window to check out the possibility, I spotted my mother rounding the corner and heading for the front door. I'm pretty sure she looked up and saw me. In my imagination it was like those eyes on a cartoon character that telescope out of their head to hyperfocus on what they're going after. I was in full panic mode.

Before I could think of what to do next, the elevator dinged, stopping on our floor. The doors opened, and my mom stepped into the hallway, cool and collected.

"Hello, Caryn."

"Hi, Ma."

I couldn't breathe.

I hatched a desperate plan in my mind. As soon as she opened the door, I'd squeeze around her, get in my room, and shovel stuff under my bed really fast while she took her coat off.

My mother found her keys and slowly unlocked the door while asking me, "How was *The Nutcracker*?"

My heart was beating wildly.

"It was great, Ma."

She slowly opened the front door, only enough for her to step in. Suddenly my very petite mother became the size of New York Giants defense player Rosey Grier. I couldn't get around her, under her, or over her.

Before I could get all the way in the front door, my mother swung open the coat closet door, cutting off my way to my room.

She was still talking to me, "Well, tell me all about *The Nutcracker*."

"It was wonderful. Really great."

"You look a little jumpy, Caryn."

I upped my bad acting job. "No, I'm not jumpy at all. Not jumpy."

As she slowly took off her coat, she asked me the dreaded question, "Did you clean your room?"

There's a Bible story about the disciple Peter swearing his forever loyalty to Jesus. Jesus pretty much smirks and says, "Before the day is over, you're gonna deny me three times." A couple hours later, soldiers cuff Jesus and take him to the high priest to be sentenced. When different folks question Peter about hanging with Jesus, good ol' Pete lies about it three times in a row, saying he never met the guy.

I went down that Peter path with my mother, already knowing it wasn't going to have a happy ending. I knew I should shake my head side to side in a "no" at my mother's question, but I ended up nodding "yes." I meant to say, "No, Ma, I didn't." Instead, I said, "Sure I did."

Without looking at me, she said, "Oh, good. I thought you would because that was part of our bargain, you know. You had to clean your room before going to the show."

And I said, "Yeah. Right. Yeah."

She took forever to close the closet door, so I tried to inch around her.

"Why are you trying to get past me?" she asked. "Just relax."

By now I could sense that she absolutely knew what really happened.

"No, I'm relaxed. I'm relaxed."

She waited a long ten seconds, then asked, "Was it hard to do?"

"What? Was what hard to do?"

"Clean your room."

At that moment the smartest thing to do would be to admit, "I didn't clean my room." But like Peter, I kept it all going.

"What do you mean?"

"Well, you cleaned your room, didn't you?"

Here was chance number two to fess up, but I didn't take it.

I said, "Yes, I did."

She said, "I'm so glad."

As she lingered another thirty seconds to hang up her coat, she moved a hanger out of the way. There, on a hook, was my brother's braided leather belt that he had made himself during a craft time in the park the previous summer.

I could see my mother's eyes on that leather belt, too, when she said to me for the third and last time, "So you cleaned your room?"

I still didn't fall on my sword. I went all in.

"Yes, I did."

And she said, "I'm so glad because I'm going to go look now."

She walked into my room and came back out right away. "It doesn't look like you cleaned your room."

But I still tried to act my way out of it. I started in with a "What-Happened-Was" story, but she was not hearing it.

She said, "No. It's too late. I'm going to do something that I really don't like doing. But the lies that you told were so obvious that you could get yourself hurt badly lying like that. So I'm going to beat your behind so that you never do that again."

She took the belt off the hook and made it memorable. It was the first time she had ever physically punished me, and it was the last time. I know it made her feel much worse than me.

Then she told me, "And if you ever decide to lie again, it better be a doozy. You better make it big and entertaining. You really need to think about this because if you get caught in a lie, there are people who won't just kick your ass, they might really want to hurt you. If your life depends on it, you better not tell lies that are that easy to disprove."

When Clyde got home later, I said, "Why did you make that belt? Asshole!"

He shrugged, "I needed a belt."

I shouted, "You must have known what was going to happen."

He said, "If you had cleaned your room, it never would have."

"Okay. Yeah. Yeah. I get it. You're Mr. Big Adult now," I said, pissed that he didn't sympathize. "You don't understand."

Later, when I thought about it, I realized he probably understood really well. Ma had probably beat his behind all over the house with that belt at some point as well, and I've got to say, Clyde was a dutiful son to our mother. Always.

I'm sure I made her mad many times. The consequences were always a low-toned verbal whooping. But this one was a lifelong lesson for me. I make a living pretending to be somebody else. When I lie in real life, and we all do sometimes, I at least make it amusing enough to be forgiven. To all you parents who think giving your kid a beating was a terrible thing, and YOU would never do such a thing, live well in your perfection. In my day that's what most parents did—if you got out of line, you were inviting a rod or a belt or a hand to visit your behind.

The next big life lesson from my mom happened about a year later when I was more interested in impressing my friends than worried about what my mom might think or do. She never forced a choice on me. She always made me choose for myself and live with the good or bad consequences.

One winter day, I was home, and my mother was out for the day. My friends all came over to my house for the afternoon. My mother had left a pack of Kool cigarettes on the kitchen counter, and we thought it would be fun to smoke cigarettes and listen to music. I didn't think about all the windows being closed because the heat was on. Seven cigarettes were lit.

Suddenly, we heard a key turning in the front door. Every one of my friends stubbed out their smokes and beat it out the front door while my mom came in, saying, "Hi, Mrs. Johnson. Bye, Mrs. Johnson."

I squinted at my mother through the haze of smoke and didn't even think about lying when she said, "Were you all smoking in here?"

I said, "Yes, Ma."

She stood quiet for a minute. I was sweating it a bit.

Then, she said, "I want you to look around you so you understand what just happened."

I looked around the now empty room, at the empty cigarette pack and the full ashtray. No doubt it was a dumb thing to do, pretty clear to me now.

She said, "When you do stuff like this with other people, they are undoubtedly going to leave you in the lurch. You'll be the one left to answer for it. When you make choices, you have to be ready to deal with it all alone."

I apologized.

Then, she turned and said, "If you're going to do something like smoke in here, at least go in the back bedroom and open the window so it's not the first thing I smell and see in here. Be smart. Pay attention, Caryn."

There was only one lie that she never caught me at.

After the hospital, she started baking again, probably because recipes made sense to her. She was a big fan of German chocolate cake, which has a gooey frosting with coconut and chopped-up pecans. She loved it. Clyde and I hated it, but we didn't have the heart to tell her. To us the frosting looked like someone had barfed and left it to dry. I could barely look at it. So when my mother wasn't looking, Clyde and I would cut off three or four pieces and throw them down the incinerator chute in the hallway. Then when we'd come home from school a week later, there would be another whole German chocolate cake she had baked.

Years and years later, I asked my mom, "Why did you always make German chocolate?"

She said, "The two of you ate so much of it I wanted you to have more of what you loved."

Only then did I admit that the cakes went, piece by piece, into the incinerator.

She was floored. She had never found that out.

Ma was much more direct with me about what she liked and didn't like. When I was a kid, she used to love a candy called Mary Jane, a rectangle of molasses-and-peanut-butter taffy, individually wrapped. It was penny candy that became hard to find in the '90s and 2000s.

Somehow, years later, I tracked down where you could still buy them in New York, and I sent my mom some whenever I could. I thought she'd love it.

One day we were talking on the phone, and she told me, "Stop sending me Mary Janes. I don't like them anymore. I'm not going to eat them."

All right, then. Order canceled.

My mother had an idea of what she thought I needed to learn and when I needed it most, even in those years when she was trying to make sense of everything herself without letting anyone know that she was lost. When I stop and think about it, she was a damn good actor herself.

Like most preteens, I was sometimes too cool to wear boots and a warm coat and hat during wintertime.

My mother would see me heading to the door, ready to go, in just a hooded sweatshirt and sneakers. She never forced me to put on a coat and boots. She'd say, "When you get really cold, don't blame me. I don't want to hear about it. You won't have time to come back home, so once we're out there, that's it. And if you get sick from making this choice, then you'll have to be okay with those consequences."

And let me tell you, I didn't like being cold or sick or both. It came down to this: Why wouldn't she want me to be warm and snug? Was she telling me something bad for me? The answer was no, and yet I still didn't get it. She used to call that "hard head, soft ass." I wish I could say I learned after I froze my butt off the first time. I didn't until the third time when I did that BS of "No, I am fine" and almost froze my toes off my foot. My mom looked at me as if to say, "You are being a dumbass," and shook her head. That head shake made it clear to me that she was right. I was a dumbass to keep doing stupid things that only harmed me. I was over it.

She really wanted me to understand that I had to be able to count on myself. And do for myself. That generation of women was sold the myth that if you're pretty and feminine, you can marry a man who would take care of you. She let me know there was no guarantee, no matter what. She would tell me quite often that it was important to make my own money and that I couldn't count on somebody else to take care of me. In lieu of, you know, waking up married to a very, very rich man, I would have to get a job and support myself.

I would listen to other women talking about money together in the hallways or outside. Usually, the conversation would sound something like this:

"I don't have to discuss with my man what I spent my money on. I earn that money myself. And he always wants half."

The other woman might reply, "Why do you have to give him half? You earn that money. You know, you pay for the groceries and the kids' shoes and all of that. What the hell does he buy?"

Even though these women could be quite dickish, they were smart enough to keep their own coin. I heard that loud and clear.

One afternoon, my mother was talking to a group of women. I was nearby and heard one of the ladies say, "You know, Caryn's no beauty. She's gonna have to find a job and work."

I think it probably hurt my mother more than it hurt me because she grew up not being the shiniest bulb in the chandelier. She looked just like me. Her cousin Arlene always got all the attention for her beauty.

Ma responded to it in a completely even and calm tone.

"Caryn knows that. She knows she doesn't look like other girls. Caryn looks like herself. Whatever she decides she wants to do, she already knows she needs to be able to support herself and get by."

I appreciate that my mother told me the truth. I still made my share of choices that didn't work out early on. But I never got in a position where I couldn't change my life because I was dependent on another person to support me. I knew I'd be able to figure it out.

Chapter Seven

You know how folks will ask, "Do you remember where you were the day Elvis died?" or, "when John Lennon was killed outside his apartment building in New York?" The list is long now, right? Famous people are popping off the planet every week. I was writing this book on the day Queen Elizabeth II checked out at age ninety-six.

I don't like to think about where I was the day my friend Robin Williams left us. I loved Robin, like millions of other people. I was lucky enough to have him as a close friend. My mother adored him, too. She loved to laugh, and not many made that happen better than Robin.

Probably the first "Do you remember . . . ?" for me was the day John F. Kennedy was shot in Dallas. I can still hear the *bing-bong-bing* sound from the school intercom system when I was in second grade. The nun teaching us stopped talking, and we all looked up at the intercom box, like God's face would be up there with an announcement. The principal came on to say that school was canceled for the rest of the day. The president of the United States had been shot.

We all quietly put on our coats, filed out of school, and started walking home. It was the first time I had ever seen that many adults crying. The teachers were weeping. The custodian was bawling. Everywhere, on the sidewalks, people were sobbing. The police officer who helped us cross the street had tears streaming down his face. I didn't understand what it all meant.

The year before, my mother, Clyde, and I went to see Kennedy when he was campaigning around New York City. It was one of the hottest days of the whole summer. Ma, Clyde, and I were on one side of a crowded parking lot, and he was standing on a small wooden platform way on the other side. He looked about a half inch tall to me.

Everything he was saying floated over my seven-year-old head. I was pretty focused on my cherry snow cone. However, it did sink in that the words, "Ask not what your country can do for you—ask what you can do for your country," meant that we were all Americans and that we needed to take care of the country.

I was too young to know that John F. Kennedy was part of the hope for the future of black folks in America. He was the first president who publicly got behind the civil rights movement, especially in the South. Martin Luther King Jr. had been arrested for peaceful protests and resistance, and Kennedy, while he was still campaigning, made the phone calls to get him released from jail and the charges dropped. Word got around, and 70 percent of black people nationwide voted Kennedy into office when the election came around.

When Martin Luther King Jr. was assassinated on his hotel room balcony in 1968, I was a teenager and old enough to understand exactly what it meant. Between Kennedy's and King's deaths, I had begun to see what was going down in other parts of the country. At first, it confused me. My New York neighborhood was so diverse that I didn't know there were other places where you couldn't mix it up with other races without being run out, beaten, or arrested. I didn't know about segregation until I saw it on TV. I had no idea people couldn't move about freely and go where they wanted to go. I was never kept out of a place or any event.

I'd watch the news and then ask my mother, "What are they doing? Why are they using fire hoses on those folks?"

She would say, "People are trying to vote, and some other people don't want that to happen."

"Do they do that here?" I asked her.

"No. We can all vote here."

It wasn't all love, peace, and understanding in New York. Civil rights uprisings were happening in Harlem and in Brooklyn, but those locations were still worlds away for me when I was a little kid. I was also never told that certain stores and places of business were known for making black people feel unwelcome. Ma wouldn't bother going into them. Plenty of others were happy to have her business.

I always knew I was black. Well, actually, I think I was considered colored when I was little, and then I think I became a negro, and when I listened to the governor of Mississippi, I heard him refer to what the niggers were trying to do in attempting to go to school with white people. Now you must remember I lived and grew up in New York City, and for the life of me, I could not understand what the problem was! I went to school with light-skinned Spanish kids and dark-skinned Puerto Rican kids, kids who had Japanese moms and white dads, and straight-up white kids. We half-ass learned that black people were enslaved in the olden days. I would question my mother about white people trying to stop black people in the South from trying to vote and attempt to wrap my head around the silliness of such a thing. Because of where I grew up, I understood that there were people really *here* in the USA who felt I was not as good as, and could never be as good as or as smart as, someone who was white. As a little kid, I knew that simply was not true.

I do remember watching the news and seeing people walking and holding signs and sometimes singing. Suddenly there would be a huge stream of water knocking them down like bowling pins, and the police would rush in and hit people with their wooden batons, hitting little children as well as adults. And here I lived among whites and blacks and Asians and Latino folks *and* the cops who escorted me across the big streets when I walked to school, who were everywhere when I was growing up. I did notice when I was little that in movies like *Gone with the Wind*, or any of the movies I had access to on *The Late Show* or *The Early Show* or *Million Dollar Movie* on Channel 9, black people were always the dancing servant or were chasing watermelon, with the exception of *Our Gang*, where there was a kind of equality among the kids. And any black person I saw on TV spoke in some strange kind of English—again, no one I knew looked or sounded like that.

I'd ask my mother, "How come all the black people were servants?"

"This is a movie," she'd answer. "It's not historical. We were a lot of different things, but this is the way some people want to tell their stories." She went on to explain that there are many stories we have not heard about the scientists, the doctors, the botanists. "Maybe when you grow up and find those stories, you can tell them."

My mother, like many black women of her generation, didn't want to get bogged down in the history of slavery. She especially didn't want Clyde and me to feel we were limited by what had happened in the past. She did explain that that's why people were marching and why it's important to know how to keep moving forward because that is how things change. She was the same way about her own personal history. She believed in perseverance and moving forward, not standing still. I know I asked her if these things had ever happened to her, and in her very Emma way, this is what she said:

"Listen, there are going to be terrible things that happen in the world. And there's nothing you can do about them. They are what they are. But your decision is going to have to be, 'Do I allow those bad things to stunt my growth as a human being? Am I just going to sit down and die over it? Or am I going to try to figure out how to be better?' Which one do you think is a waste of time?"

My mother didn't have time to waste time. She had to figure out how to get by and get us raised. And she *never* answered the question!

She found her next job outside our apartment door. The projects often had a children's playground outside, and somehow the city decided to demolish ours and build a nursery school. Well, all the mothers protested—picket signs, the whole kit and caboodle—without success. Once the school was built, there were jobs to be had, and my mother applied for one of them and got hired! And don't for a minute think I didn't tease her . . . at arm's length!

In the '60s, a new preschool program was launched called Head Start. Many people felt if we could get to little kids early enough, we could possibly give them a stronger start in life, which turns out to be true. Just ask the folks at *Sesame Street*. My mother was hired as an assistant to the nursery school teachers. It turns out she was a pretty good teacher. Once the powers that be got to know her, they saw how effectively she worked with those open little minds. They felt that she had the makings of a great teacher. So they funded her college education at Hunter College, then at New York University to get a degree in early education.

She took the opportunity given and eventually went all the way through to getting her master's degree. Clyde and I were older then, and she counted on us to stay out of trouble while she went to classes.

I remember her riding her electric bicycle off to her college graduation, her gown billowing out behind her. I don't know why she didn't want Clyde and me there, but that was how she was. She never wanted to interrupt anybody else's day.

One time my mother and I were talking, and she laughed and shook her head, saying, "When they were going to build that preschool, I was one of the people out there on the street protesting it because it took away your playground. And here it became my way to get an advanced education and career. You never know what's possible."

My mother had been raised to be a decent person, the same way Arlene had been raised, but she always felt that kids should be heard as individuals and not grouped together. She was more interested in a child figuring out who they were instead of how they fit in. My mom preferred the honesty and open-mindedness of children to the company of other adults who had their opinions of everything set in permanent cement.

She was a really great teacher. Even now, I'll get notes

and emails from people in their forties telling me that my mother was their Head Start teacher and that they'll never forget her because of how she influenced them as kids.

Probably some of the parents will never forget her either. She had a way of teaching naturally that was very progressive for the time. She showed these little kids through demonstration how life goes.

Every year, during the last week of October, she would help the kids carve up some pumpkins. She taught them how to make a pumpkin look like a face, and they all had a great time. On Halloween, she'd put candles in the pumpkins and turn out the lights so the children could see the full effect.

Halloween would come and go, and Ma would leave the pumpkins all set up on the window ledges in the room.

A week would go by, and some of the parents would ask, "Are you going to throw those pumpkins away now?"

And Ma would only answer, "Not yet."

The parents would laugh uncomfortably and leave.

A week later, someone would ask her, "Are you really going to leave those pumpkins there?"

And she would say, "Yes. I am."

They'd shake their heads and leave.

Finally, near Thanksgiving someone would say to

her, "We would all like for you to get rid of these pump-kins now."

Ma would stop what she was doing and ask, "What's making you all so uncomfortable here?"

The parent would answer, "They're rotting. Why leave them up?"

"I have a reason. I'm trying to show the kids that this happens to everything in life: pumpkins, plants, gold-fish, birds, animals, and also people. As the pumpkins have been aging, I explain that even human beings, like grandmas and grandpas, come to a place where they are done. But it doesn't have to be scary. It's not anything to be afraid of."

The parents were taken aback. It was such a simple way to help children understand that this happens to all living things on this planet, and there is no reason to be afraid. You can be sad . . . but you need not be afraid. They may have thought her a little different, but they understood that she didn't want life to be a scary mys-tery to her students.

In retrospect, maybe her experiences made her a better teacher. She wanted the children she helped to reach their potential and face their destinies with a pos-itive and smart attitude.

My mother was always okay with knowing that people

will leap to conclusions, often out of ignorance about the big picture. She was amazingly forgiving that way.

When I was younger, people would say to me, "Why do you sound so white?"

And I'd say, "What do you mean? I sound like me. I sound like my family. I speak like my mother."

"Well," they would say, "she doesn't sound black." My mother had great diction and was a woman who championed the idea of having limitless ways of speaking and a vast vocabulary, but if you spoke to her over the phone, you could not detect color in her voice.

I'd ask, "What do you mean, 'she doesn't sound black?' What does it mean to sound black?"

One time I asked my mother, "Why do you think people keep saying to me that we don't sound black?"

My mother shrugged and said, "I haven't the slightest idea."

"They act like the way I talk is wrong."

"Ah, well, it's their problem, not your problem. It's not my problem. It's their problem."

This is the other thing people would say as if it were some kind of miracle: "Oh, you're so articulate."

I finally took a page out of Emma's book. I'd ask them a question instead of giving a response: "What do you mean? More articulate than who?"

They would stumble around for an explanation. "Well, you don't talk like . . . you know . . . you don't sound like . . . like . . ."

I'd say, "Who? I don't sound like who?"

Finally, they'd choke out, "Well, you don't sound black."

Without being an asshole, I'd ask them, "So, you're basically telling me that you don't know any black people? Is that what you're saying?"

I'd tell my mother about this, and she'd respond, "Be forgiving. They don't know any better."

I'd say, "They act surprised that you took us to hear music, see shows, museums, the movies, all of it."

And my mother would tell me, "You have to understand. They don't know anybody like you. They can't imagine that you know about art, music, world history . . . anything. This is not your problem. This is a look inside what's lacking in their world, not yours. The only people that they know who are like you either work for them or are people they only know in passing. They aren't having conversations with those people."

I would still feel annoyed that I had to deal with it.

"You have to try to be a little more understanding of their ignorance. You can spend the whole time being pissed off at their inabilities or just help them understand how it all works and why they shouldn't talk to you in that manner." My mother felt that getting angry was not going to help. She was right, it turns out.

I've met non-white people today who don't know much about being underrepresented in television and film. Who didn't know how easy it was for people to look through you or refuse to allow you in a hospital or a swimming pool. As I grew up, things on many fronts began to change slowly. There were moments in the movies that stood out dramatically in the history of race relations at the time.

I once sat in the RKO movie theater between my mother and Clyde to watch *In the Heat of the Night*, starring Sidney Poitier and Rod Steiger. Sidney plays a cop out of Chicago who ends up in a tiny southern town. Rod Steiger plays the typical white sheriff wanting to know why Sidney is there, why he's so well dressed, and why he has so much money in his wallet. Sidney explains that he is a cop from Chicago, and he has so much money because he earned it. When asked what he is called, he says, "They call me MR. TIBBS." Now it turns out there has been a murder of a white man. The sheriff discovers everything he has said is true, and Sidney reluctantly agrees to help find the killer. So they go to see another white man to gather information, and when Sidney P. addresses the man, he is so taken aback that he slaps Sidney in the face. Sidney looks at him as if to say, "Are you crazy?" and Sidney slaps him back. Baby, the whole audience gasped and then fell silent. It was called the "slap heard 'round the world."

Clyde and I both knew how much my mother loved and respected Sidney Poitier, especially after one particular bus ride in the Upper East Side of Manhattan.

We must have gone uptown for an event or performance, and we were riding the bus home. My mother was sitting by the bus window, I was in the middle, and my brother was on the aisle. Mom was always very well dressed if we went out, very put together. My brother was looking sharp in his Robert Hall suit and hat. And I was wearing my Kate Greenaway dress from Macy's with my little white lace-trimmed socks and patent leather Mary Janes.

We were riding along when suddenly I saw the bottom of my mother's yellow satin shoes because she was kneeling on the seat and leaning out of the bus window.

She screamed, "Oh, my God! Sidney! Mr. Poitier!" She was waving wildly toward the sidewalk.

I had never seen my mother do something like this in my whole childhood so far. I looked at my brother.

He was astonished. He looked at me. I was astonished. We both looked over at her because as quickly as that happened, she turned around, sat down on the seat, and adjusted her skirt like nothing at all had happened.

I looked back over at Clyde like, *Did Ma just scream out of a bus window?* He gave me an eye signal to mean, *Do not say or do anything. You'll get us in trouble.*

Clyde and I might have talked about it more between us later, but we never brought it up to our mother.

Years later, at an awards show, I had the chance to meet Sidney Poitier. As we talked, I told him the story of the three of us on the bus and my mother yelling out the window to him and what a shock it was to two kids who had never seen their mom lose her composure. He found the story charming and told me to bring her over to meet him if she was ever at an event.

About a year later, I was hosting a benefit evening that Sidney Poitier was kind enough to attend. My mother was with me.

I brought my mother over to meet him, saying, "Sidney, I'd like to introduce my mother. Ma, this is Sidney Poitier."

My mother was the queen of elegance, extending her hand and saying, "So very honored to meet you, Mr. Poitier."

Sidney said, "I love Whoopi. She's such a great—Wait . . . Have we met?"

My mother said, "Oh, no, we haven't. I certainly would have remembered."

"Oh. You look so very familiar."

"No," Ma said. "I would have remembered meeting you."

Sidney started to talk again and then said, "Wait. Were you on a city bus?"

My mother looked over at me, and I knew I had fucked up.

She stayed dignified and said, "Oh, I see. Caryn has told you that story. No. We have never met, but it's been a pleasure to meet you now, Mr. Poitier. Will you please excuse me?"

She headed to the ladies' room, and I said to Sidney, "I think I really messed up telling you that story."

"Well, it was a wonderful story. I hope she didn't think I was rude."

"No. No. It was my fault. I think I embarrassed her. I'm going to go find out."

Sidney wanted me to bring her back, but I knew that wouldn't happen.

When I went into the ladies' room, she wouldn't

look at me or speak to me. She simply said, "I'd like to go now."

I said, "Yes, okay, I need to say good night."

And without looking at me, she said, "I'll wait in the car."

It was a week before she would speak to me again. When she finally did, she asked me, "Why would you do that? You really embarrassed me in front of Mr. Poitier."

"But, Ma. He loved the story and he loved meeting you."

"Caryn, you must be careful and think through things before you tell stories about other people."

I apologized, but she still had nothing else to say to me for another three weeks.

It was hard on me, too. I couldn't stand the thought of hurting my mother.

Years later, she admitted that she might have overreacted in the moment. She explained that it was still early in my career, things were happening for me, and she didn't want anyone to see her as being a laughingstock.

I tried to assure her that Sidney thought she was charming and no one was laughing at her.

She said, "It doesn't matter. That's how I saw Mr. Poitier as seeing me."

I could understand that. I promised to do better.

As much as my mother loved the movies, I think it meant a lot for her to see Sidney Poitier become one of the first black actors to have leading roles and become the first black actor to win the Academy Award for Best Actor in 1964. Barriers were starting to crumble, and Mr. Poitier was moving us into the future.

In the fall of 1966, when I was ten, I tuned in for the premiere of a new outer-space show on TV. I liked everything sci-fi, so I was sure to watch *Star Trek*. I jumped off the couch and ran to get Ma when I saw that a black actress, Nichelle Nichols, was playing the part of Lieutenant Uhura, the communications officer on the *Enterprise*. I completely lost my mind over it. I had never seen any black people in any science fiction show, not even in the background walking down the street or driving by. She was the first black person I had seen in a show about the future. (The next black actress to play a professional woman didn't happen again until 1968 when Diahann Carroll starred in *Julia*.)

I had the chance to be in the company of Nichelle Nichols a few times during my career. She was a gutsy and impressive advocate for black people to be in positions of authority in entertainment. I had to tell her, "To me, as a little kid, you let me know that black people would be around in the future. We'd have a place there, too."

When Gene Roddenberry, creator of the original *Star Trek*, was in the process of creating *Star Trek: The Next Generation* in the late 1980s, I gave him a call. I told him I'd like to play a part in the new series and asked if he could see if there was a role for me.

He asked me why, and I said it matters to me that black people be seen in the future. I told him that you couldn't find black people in science fiction of the past before *Star Trek*. He couldn't believe that, so I challenged him to take a look for himself.

Two days later, he called my house and said, "I need you to come in and meet with me."

I said, "Okay," and I went.

Gene told me, "First of all, I'm going to build you a character for this new series. I've got her in my mind. But it turns out, you're right. I couldn't find black people in science fiction. I had no idea."

He went on to explain that on the original *Star Trek*, he had created a world in which everyone was living. And he said, "I guess I didn't understand so well that what I was doing had never been done before."

This is why my mother told me to be forgiving of what people don't know and help them understand instead of walking away mad. The thing is, when you're looking at something like a television show and you always see someone who looks like you, then you don't notice what else is missing. You only notice when what's always missing is you.

In 2022, the world lost both Sidney Poitier and Nichelle Nichols. I'm going to guess that neither of them would want to be remembered for the day they died unless how they lived is included. A whole lot of change happened because of them before that day. Attention must be paid.

A picture of my mother as a teenager, visiting her grandmother in Jacksonville, Florida.

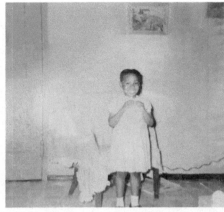

Me, around age five, in our living room in the Chelsea projects.

Me and my brother, Clyde, on Easter Sunday at our grandad's apartment in Harlem. The camera was a gift from our grandfather to Clyde, who took pictures till the day he died.

Me in all my cuteness.

My mother at her nursing school graduation, 1954
(second row, fourth from the right).

My mother, Emma
Harris Johnson.

One of my mother's Head Start classes and a visiting baby.

One of my mother's Head Start classes with the other two teachers in the class, Lily and Evelyn. These women were truly amazing, and from time to time someone will tell me, beaming, they were in my mother's class. I love it.

Emma at the White House.

Emma just chilling at the St. James's Club in LA.

My mother, dressed and ready to go out and about. This was taken in the apartment I rented while I was doing my Broadway show, *Whoopi Goldberg*.

Screenshots from a video of my mother taken by my brother, whom I was directing over the phone. They were both living in Berkeley, California, at the time. Shoot a bit of video of your loved ones while you can. It will help when you least expect it.

My mom and me, brunching at the hotel formally known as the St. James's Club, now called the Sunset Tower.

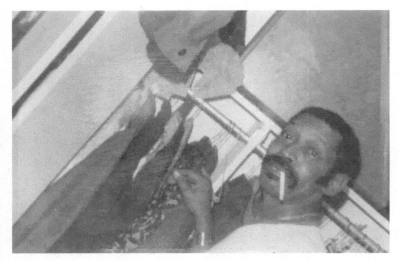

Robert Johnson, my pop.

My brother, Clyde Keith Johnson. A sports fanatic and baseball coach who went to church often, never cursed, taught me how to be a good sister, and *loved* nothing more than to get in the car and drive down to NYC. He loved driving through America.

Clyde and me at a Jets game. We used to go to *any* basketball game we could find. Clyde looked like Michael Jordan, and when Jordan was playing, those were some of the best times . . .

Me, Clyde, my mother, and Aunty Ruth (I told you about her miniature Louisville Slugger; she is my cousin Arlene's mother). This was taken at the Pink House, which once belonged to David Niven, during one of my wedding preparations when I lived in the Palisades in LA.

Chapter Eight

Some folks will ask me, "Whoopi, you wear a white button-up shirt almost every day. Why's that?"

See, I don't care what I wear, as long as it's comfortable. A white button-up shirt seems like an easy solution to looking okay when I'm in public. It looks and feels clean.

And now that I think about it, maybe it has something to do with the fact that I wore one every single school day as a kid—I went to Catholic school. That's at least 1,600 days of wearing a uniform to get to the eighth grade. By the end of kindergarten, you kind of no longer give a shit about what you're wearing. It was always the same: a white button-up shirt and a plaid skirt.

I went to a whole lot of Mass as a child. I had to go. It was required of kids going to St. Columba Catholic

School. I genuflected my way through grammar school.
We all would head out on Sunday morning for church,
and we didn't eat meat on Fridays either. None of that
made sense to me, but I knew that as soon as I got older,
I was not going to church anymore. There were quite a
few places of worship in the neighborhood, and going
into these different places to hear that not everyone be-
lieves the same thing or way was a good thing for us
because it allowed us to ask questions. Though it was
annoying for some of the teachers.

My family didn't know it at the time, but I went
through grade school with dyslexia, never having a name
for it. I have zero memory of any educational triumphs.
Mostly, I tried to get through. I learned the Ten Commandments, but when I was seven, they made sense to
me in their original form. You know, on those stone tab-
lets Moses hauled down the mountainside. Before the
church wrote out its own definitions for each one, the
original version was a good life guide.

Like the eighth commandment, "Don't steal." Seems
clear to me. Somebody is going to pay for it, and you
didn't legit get it. Go get your own.

Number six is pretty unquestionable: "Thou shalt
not kill." Nobody wants to leave this incarnation once
they arrive in full form. Leave them be.

"Don't bear false witness against your neighbor."
You know how it is with trash talk about other people:
"They're bad; you're good." "They're idiots; you're a
genius." "They suck; you're normal." It's a vicious circle.
They're thinking the same shit about you. So, commandment number nine is like today's STFU! Keep it
to yourself. Maybe they will, too.

I've got to say, nobody made a bigger impression on
me about how to share the earth with other people than
my mother. But it was never through any rules or labels
of what was sin and what wasn't. She was far more subtle.
She was determined to make me decide for myself, to
come to my own conclusions about how to be.

I had a friend, Robert, when I was in grammar school.
He was different, no doubt. He was bottom-heavy and
had pimples on his face, but he was a good kid, smart
and kind. There was a small group of us that fit that category, different from the other kids. I felt like I got Robert
and he got me. So, we hung out and talked.

Once, our school got to take a daylong field trip
somewhere, and my mother volunteered to be one of
the chaperones that came with us. On that day, I was
one of the popular kids. I was talking it up with everybody and feeling happy.

When we got home later that evening, I was really

excited about where we'd been, and I was strutting and feeling my shit about my day.

My mother looked at me and said, "You had a good time today, didn't you?"

I said, "Yeah, I did. I had a really good time. I'm really happy. I was, you know, talking to lots of people and hanging out."

"Oh. Yeah, I saw that," she said. "Were some of them the same girls that made you cry a couple weeks back?"

"Yeah, they were," I said. "But it's better now because we are all friends."

"Oh, I see. I wonder if Robert feels like that."

"What? If Robert feels like what?"

"Well, kind of happy and kind of glad that he was able to fit in."

I got really quiet. I realized that I might not have been nice to Robert on the trip. I may have even laughed at him a bit, like the other popular kids did that day. I didn't pull him into the group like a friend would do.

That started to eat me up. We were friends, and I somehow didn't respect that I needed to be his friend when other people were looking, too.

I went from strutting to hanging my head for how I had treated Robert.

Ma said to me, "I didn't say this to make you feel

bad. I said this so that you will remember what this feels like, when you make somebody feel bad like I think you might have made Robert feel today."

When she held that up to me, I really wanted to go in the corner, get into a box, and close the lid because it was a terrible feeling.

I knew what it felt like to be the one left out. I'd been there myself, more than once. You know, everybody loves you when you have something they want. They're all your friends when you're flush with candy. After the candy's gone, they'll say something like, "Stay here. We have to go do something and we'll be right back."

Then an hour later, you realize you're one duped eight-year-old and those friends aren't coming back.

Ma would say to me, "You didn't like it when somebody did it to you. You have to remember what this feels like or you'll always be walking into walls."

I'm really glad that I got all of that from her early on in my life because it does shade how I am now.

I always say if it's not in the Ten Commandments, then it's nothing to worry about. The rules are right there. Jesus even packaged it all into one flat statement: "Do unto others as you'd have them do unto you." Meaning, don't mess with people if you don't want them to mess with you. Don't hurt other people. Just don't. That's what I try to live by now the best I can because it was my mom's approach to life, which is pretty remarkable, considering she had probably gone through a lot of shit in the hospital for two years.

I never heard my mother yell at anyone, before or after that time. She wasn't a yeller. I could tell when she was angry, though. Her face would change, and the sun would go down. It would get a little dark and chilly. But she wouldn't ever yell or strike out in any way. She'd remove herself from the scene.

She would tell me and Clyde never to initiate a fight. She'd say, "Don't swing on anyone, even a man. You can't be sure he won't swing back on you."

But she'd also say that if somebody else got up in my face and swung at me, I'd better fight back until I could get away. She was very much about not starting shit, but she also knew that "turning the other cheek" wasn't going to help if somebody came at you.

She didn't impose her beliefs on anyone else. She accepted that people have different realities, and as long as theirs didn't get in her personal space, she was good, doing her own thing.

She met enough people in the early parts of her life to know that there were a lot of good people, a lot of kind people in the world. She let me know that people will give each other a hand if you let them know what you need somehow. That's how it was in the projects when I was little. There might be someone out of work or having a tough month. Folks would figure out how to get that person a box full of things they needed to get by. Or somebody would show up out of the blue and say, "Hey, do you want this extra (whatever) that I have?"

My mom believed that if you knew someone needed something and you were able to help them out, then you should. And if somebody helps you out, you should pay it forward. Help somebody else out.

She believed in the humanity of people because, at the time, in the 1960s, things were changing. Women were standing up for their rights, including things as simple as opening a bank account without a husband. My mom was out there with her placards on sticks, making her statements along with the other marching women.

They all faced blowback from folks who held the traditional beliefs that women shouldn't make their own decisions, have jobs, and choose how to take care of themselves. My mother's attitude was if you're hungry, if you need a roof over your head, if you have kids to take care of, then you do what you have to do. You do the work, whatever that might be. She was very nonjudgmental about many things, mostly about other people.

When I became an adult, I had several friends who worked in the sex business.

One day, one of them said to Ma, "Do I make you uncomfortable because, you know, this is what I do for a living?"

"Why would you make me feel uncomfortable?" my mom asked in return, the way she always did, answering a question with another question.

My friend said, "Well, I didn't want to stay if it bothers you."

She said, "No. I'm fine with what you do, unless you start shooting ping-pong balls at me from your vaginal area. That could make me a little uncomfortable. Other than that, I think we're fine."

Some women in the projects treated my mom with a cold shoulder. She wasn't like them. She wouldn't gossip or talk trash about anybody else.

She would spend her time writing, reading, or teaching herself to play piano. My mom seemed to be fine on her own, doing things her way, so some of the other women acted suspicious of her.

I'm sure there was much more drama with these women that I wasn't privy to as a child. But my mother never talked about it. She had her tight circle of friends: her cousin Arlene and a few others that lived nearby. She didn't need to be popular. Ever.

When I was rehearsing my first Broadway show, these same women had the attitude toward my mom like, "*You're* the one who ended up with a famous kid? *You?*"

Then, when the show opened, a lot of those women suddenly started coming around, saying, "Oh, my God, I can't believe this is happening! Good for Caryn! I would really like to see her show."

My mom called me and said, "Is it wrong for me to ask for six tickets?"

"No. I don't think it's a problem," I said. "I've been told I have house seats. I can give you those seats. Who did you want to bring?"

She named the women she was bringing.

I said, "Are you kidding me? Why would you give any tickets to those women?"

"Listen, it's very important that I bring them to the theater. It's very important that I be the person I hope I am."

So I said, "Okay."

She told me, "This is going to happen for a couple of more weeks, just so you know."

She brought them to the theater in groups of four or

five so they could see the show for free. Afterward, they would come backstage, and then my mother would go out with them and have white wine. She would laugh and drink with these women who had broken her heart for twenty-seven years. She never let on that there was a problem.

Suddenly they all decided they wanted to be good friends with my mother. Everybody wanted to hang out with her.

That's when she responded, "Well, it's really not me. It's not what I do. But it's good you got to see Caryn's show. I'm so glad you could join us."

They got the message.

My mother, who could have taken the last swing, went on her way without them.

She showed me how to do that kind of thing, to be okay with myself when I was a teenager.

I have a friend, Rosie, who was my friend forever, starting in grade school. As a teenager, I started dressing like a hippie because I liked the look. I wore overalls and faded work shirts and Afro puffs on my head.

One day we were going to the movies together. Rosie stopped at the door and said, "I think you should change your clothes."

"Why?" I asked. "I'm okay like this."

She told me, "We're going to the theater."

"So? I don't want to change my clothes. I think I'm fine."

Rosie looked away from me.

"What's the matter?" I asked.

She hesitated and then said, "You just look like you're dirty."

"But I'm not. You know that."

She turned around. "Maybe we shouldn't go to the movies today."

I said, "Okay. Fine."

Then she left.

I said to my mother, "Was I wrong?"

And she said, "I don't know. Were you?"

"Why me? Why wasn't she going to change?"

"Because she thought she was clean, and she didn't feel you were clean. So, she gave you a choice."

"Well, what do you think?"

"It doesn't matter what I think," my mother said. "It matters what you think and feel about something."

The nuns who were my teachers in grammar school taught that there was right and there was wrong. And you didn't want to do wrong because it was a sin and, depending on how bad it was, God was going to punish you.

My mom taught me something even more effective.

She taught me to make choices on my own that nobody else could make for me. Then I had to live with however those choices made me feel. I had to stand up. I couldn't pretend I didn't know what I was doing. I didn't have to fear punishment from God. I only had to think about whether I could live with myself and my choices.

Because of her, I was always me. I followed how I felt. She wouldn't even let me hitch on to her opinion of God.

One time, I asked her, "Do you believe in God?"

She lit one of her More cigarettes and said, "Who wants to know?"

"Me. No one else. I'm asking."

She said, "Yes. But who are you asking for?"

I was like, "Ma, I'm asking for me."

"Are you? Are you sure?"

"Yes, Ma. I'm pretty sure."

"Okay," she said. "Because sometimes, you know, we ask questions because we want guidance to hide in instead of thinking for ourselves."

I said, "No, I just wondered if you believe in God."

"Well, I believe in my God."

And I said, "Is your God different from other people's God?"

She said, "I think, yes, sometimes."

She was thoughtful. Yeah. You know, she was really

thoughtful. She didn't rush her judgments or her answers. She didn't expect God to drop in and rescue us or think that we got to blame him for whatever mess humans get themselves into.

Her attitude was if you believe in God, then you have to believe that God is really smart and made us smart enough to know how to maneuver through this life.

Chapter Nine

I'm at an age and stage in my career where I get asked, "Is there a part you'd still like to play?"

I've got an answer.

A monster.

That usually gets a raised eyebrow.

I'm not talking about a female villain or a monster bitch mother-in-law type. It's not a metaphor, you know. I want to play an actual monster.

Horror movies are in my DNA. I like 'em. They make me happy. No slasher films. I don't want to be scared by anything like reality. Give me a good ol' Dracula movie or some giant Japanese reptile terror.

When I was a kid, we had *Chiller Theatre* on our TV every Saturday night. WPIX, Channel 11 in New York. The host was John Zacherle, this guy with a sunken-in face and weird eyes, dressed all in black. He was fantastic and the scariest man I'd ever seen. He would introduce the movie of the night and then come back on at the commercial breaks. The breaks were done live, so you never knew what was going to happen with him.

My mom, Clyde, and I would make up our Jiffy Pop popcorn before the opening credits of the show, which showed this gray and dead-looking hand coming up through the dry desert ground.

Godzilla, *The Crawling Eye*, *Mothra*, *The Wolf Man*, and things like giant leeches falling from New York skyscrapers completely captured me. I didn't even know these movies were called horror. I thought they were good entertainment that happened to be scary.

The famous Hammer horror movies also rolled out when I was young: *Dracula: Prince of Darkness*, *The Plague of the Zombies*, *Kiss of the Vampire*, *The Gorgon*, all the really good ones. We'd go see them first at the RKO theater on the corner of Twenty-Third Street and Eighth Avenue; then a few years later, they'd show up on TV. I still scour the TV listings every week to see if any of them are playing.

Yeah, the plotlines can be ridiculous. But they'd still get you jumping. You get that all-over feeling of knowing you're going to be surprised or shocked. Like in *Trilogy of Terror*: Karen Black gets attacked by a wooden doll that is about fourteen inches tall. It's a tribal Zuni hunter doll that comes to life and attacks her legs with a knife as she walks through her living room. Then it hacks its way through her locked bedroom door to get to her, making croaky animal sounds. At some point, it seems ridiculous that she is locked in her own apartment and can't seem to open a window and toss the doll out, but that's how it is and you just have to go with it. Seems like an ugly doll with pointy teeth coming to life couldn't scare the shit out of you, but it does.

Same with seeing *Jaws* in the movie theater when I was a teenager. At first, I remember thinking, *Oh, my God, I'm seeing a movie about a shark?* Then, there was the music, like a heart thumping, and you see the girl's legs kicking underwater, and you know there's a big-ass shark scoping her out. You can't catch your breath. Your hair feels like it's lifting off your head. You want to yell, but you can't. That's some good shit. In fact, I bet I'm not the only one who won't get in the ocean over my knees anymore.

Then there were the Hercules movies with bodybuilder Steve Reeves as the main character. You know, when you can wrap chains around Roman columns and pull down the whole building with your muscles, well . . . that's some impressive shit. I liked that he could stop injustice with those impressive biceps.

Besides *Chiller Theatre* and TV sitcoms and variety shows, *Million Dollar Movie* was broadcast on WOR-TV Channel 9. The same movie would play all day long on Saturday starting at 9:00 a.m. Since my mom, Clyde, and I were all movie buffs, we loved it. I'd watch the same movie three times in a row if I could get away with it.

They would run the full spectrum of different kinds of movies, from *King Kong* to *Yankee Doodle Dandy*. I would sit there and absorb everything, the way it all worked. I'd see Greta Garbo, Charles Boyer, or Katharine Hepburn acting in one movie, and then they'd play someone completely different, maybe with a different accent, in another movie.

I knew about great TV shows like *I Love Lucy* and *The Danny Kaye Show*. I knew early on that acting was what I wanted to do. Then it seemed like a great thing to do. It was magic.

When I was growing up, I also got to discover what it means to be a performer playing yourself by watching the great comedians do their thing. I was absorbing it all from the pros: Moms Mabley, Totie Fields, Alan King, and Don Rickles. They made me laugh really hard.

I don't know if anyone ever asked my mother what

she wanted to do when she was a kid. It was probably not something folks asked kids in that generation. There were fewer options. I think my mom decided for herself that if she had children, she would do it differently; whatever they were into, she would make sure conversations would happen where she could find out more. She felt that children should be heard all the time and their wishes adhered to at least some of the time.

Because my mom was open to it and encouraged it, I started going on stage around age eight at the Hudson Guild Theatre in Chelsea. The shows were performed in the auditorium of the nearby community service center, so I could get myself there and back home. It's about all I really loved doing. They had both children's theater productions and adult productions with children performing. I liked the idea that I could be anybody from anywhere at any time period. I adored that. And I love telling stories.

After doing a few plays with the Hudson Guild, I auditioned for other things. As a young teenager, I auditioned for a part in a play directed by Vinnette Carroll, who was the first black woman to direct a play on Broadway. She was also a playwright and the artistic director of the Urban Arts Corps, which she started up in the '60s.

After I auditioned, she cast me. I found out I had

the role on a Monday. Then, Vinnette called my house on Tuesday.

"I'm so sorry, darling," she said. "I've changed my mind. I feel I have to do it this way."

I suddenly no longer had the part.

When my mother came home from work, I had to explain to her about Vinnette's call.

She said, "What? What happened?"

I didn't have an answer. I didn't know what had happened, and I guess I was too crushed to ask.

I was surprised Ma was upset, but she was. She took herself over to Vinnette Carroll's theater space and had some type of conversation.

Nothing changed. I still didn't have the part. Someone Vinnette had hoped to put in the role finally showed up to audition after she had given me the part.

My mother sat with me at the kitchen table.

"There will be something else for you. You weren't expecting this, but there will be other things. You just have to keep at it."

I got to learn this knockdown lesson years before I started a film career, so it was good in the long run. Because if you're going to be an actor, at some point this kind of thing happens to you. And most of the time, nobody tells you why. You just have to keep going.

As I headed into high school, it became clear that I couldn't learn in the ways being taught.

At first, Ma would give me a look like, *Come on, you can do this.*

But then she accepted that it wasn't that I didn't want to do it; I couldn't.

When I was finishing up tenth grade, I told her I didn't want to go back. I knew this wouldn't be what she wanted to hear because she was a teacher, but she listened to me.

"If you think this is what you need to do. I don't like it," she told me, "but I know you probably wouldn't be doing it if you could figure out a way to get through."

It was harder every day. She knew I was serious about it because I was telling her upfront.

"Okay," she said. "You're not sneaking around, not going to school. You're telling me now. So, if you leave high school, we'll have to make a deal."

Education and learning were too important to my mom for her to be concerned about what I would be doing if I wasn't in school. I knew she would have to make it better for her, somehow.

She then told me, "We'll look and find things that might be of interest to you. But you have to spend some time at a lecture or an exhibit, and you have to spend time learning every week."

So this was what we would do. On Sunday, she and I would sit down with the local newspapers, and she would look up what was going on in New York. I'd have a pen and paper, and she'd read out options to me of things I might like to do.

"Okay, there's a lecture on civil rights at the library on Tuesday. And the museum of modern history has an exhibit and lecture on Thursday morning you could go to."

I'd pick out five or ten free lectures or exhibits each week and promise her that I would attend to supplement my education. That was our deal, and I stuck to it for a couple of years.

During those years, once my school uniform days were over, I found a way to look like myself. The hippies had come to Chelsea, and wearing a bra was never something I was interested in doing anyway. I would get painter pants and overalls from the surplus stores and wear long underwear shirts and multicolored tams over my natural hair. Ma was cool with whatever I wanted to wear, but I think getting used to natural hair took her a while.

A lot of the younger folks in the neighborhood, both women and men, suddenly started wearing Afros. Nobody really talked about it. It just started to happen.

But it took a while. Before, people in my mother's generation were raised to believe that they needed to look more like white people because somehow our natural hair was not attractive. You know, they'd have to explain to people about their hair. As I mentioned earlier, when my mom was working at the hospital, she straightened her hair every day. She put an iron comb in the open flame on the stove, and she would put that comb in her hair with a little Royal Crown hair grease and make it straight. That's just the way it was. But slowly, things started to shift.

There were "Black Is Beautiful" posters all over New York in the late '60s and early '70s, and James Brown was singing about being proud to be black. I think that it was never a concern in our house whether we were beautiful or not. We just were. We didn't have those kinds of discussions.

One day, I came out of the bathroom wearing my hair in a short Afro.

My mother looked at me. "Where are you going?"

I said I was going downstairs.

"So, are we having that discussion now about your hair? Are you making a statement with this look?"

Now truth be told, I just wanted to try it. I mean, lots of people had started to wear it, and I thought it looked nice. I hadn't asked her anything about my new look. I was just doing it. And she wanted to have a discussion about it.

But when I stopped to listen to what she had to say, she dropped it. "Never mind. You have every right to go out and be seen the way you want to be seen. So, if you're comfortable with what's on your head, I'm not gonna say anything more."

About a year later, she was wearing her hair in a short Afro and happy as hell not to have to use a hot comb anymore.

For the most part, she thought I should wear whatever made me feel like myself.

I once saw a movie with Peter Sellers that came out when I was young called *The World of Henry Orient*. He plays a famous, quirky New York pianist who is stalked by two teenage girls who have a crush on him. One of the teen girls wears an open fur coat wherever she goes. I dug the look and found one for myself at a thrift store. I think it was sixteen bucks, so I had to put it on hold. As odd as a fur coat would look over painter pants, Ma walked me over to the store and paid for the rest.

About fifteen years later, when I had finished filming *The Color Purple*, I wanted to give my mom something she had always wanted. I finally had some money to make it happen for her.

One day I said to her, "What have you always wanted that you never ever thought that you would get?"

She said, "Really? Why are you asking me this?"

I said, "Ma, I want to know! What did you always know that you had to have one day?"

She had an answer: "Well, I always wanted a beaver bowler."

I said, "Uh, what's that?"

She repeated it, as if I hadn't heard her. "A beaver bowler."

"I don't know what that is."

My mother gave me a look and continued, "You know what a bowler hat is, don't you?"

"Yes."

"Well, this is a bowler made out of beaver pelt. And it comes in a hat box with a brush to keep it in good shape."

You've got to remember that this was the early '80s, years before PETA was campaigning to end fur as fashion. Beaver bowlers weren't a big fashion item in the US, so I had one shipped in from Europe for my mom. She wore that hat all the time.

The other thing she told me she really wanted was an ermine coat. Ermine is one of the most luxurious furs. I was happy to get it for her, but I never saw her wear it out of the house, even in the early '80s.

One day I was walking past her bedroom, and I saw the coat laid out on the end of her bed.

"Ma, what are you going to do with the ermine coat? Why don't you wear it?"

She said, "I didn't want it to wear it."

"Okay," I said. "So, what are you going to do with it?"

That's when she showed me. She told me to go downstairs into the entryway of my LA house. I did.

Then she came to the top of the stairs with her fur coat in one hand, hanging down to the floor. She put her other hand on the railing and slowly walked down the stairs, dragging the fur coat, step by step, behind her.

I busted out laughing. We had probably watched a hundred films from the 1930s on *Million Dollar Movie* where the star—Greta Garbo, Carole Lombard, Marlene Dietrich, or Bette Davis—would slowly descend a staircase, her fur coat sweeping the steps behind her.

When the early '90s rolled around and people were throwing paint on women wearing fur coats, my mother was pissed.

She said, "These poor women had one chance to own a fur coat. And here comes somebody throwing paint on it."

She knew herself well. She said she was never going to give anybody an opportunity to toss paint on her prized coat. She said if it happened, there would for sure be a fight.

So instead she used it as a throw on her bed, and every once in a while, she'd gracefully drag it down the stairs to the first floor. My mother may not have been an actress, but she sure knew how to work it!

Chapter Ten

When the car crossed the state line from New York to New Jersey, I thought, *What am I doing?* I was having big doubts, but I kept them to myself.

I was riding in the back seat with my kid, Alexandrea, who was a toddler, heading to Texas and then eventually to California. In the front seat were two guys, both actors, one that I knew pretty well. He had been in *Long Day's Journey into Night* at a theater where my mom was working as a house manager. He was a good guy, and we would hang out together.

One day he said to me, "I've got a son about the same age as your daughter. Would you ever consider moving to the West Coast? To California?"

The idea was for me to go with him to be a nanny for our kids while he did acting jobs. I saw it as my way to get to California, a place I had always wanted to go. I was picturing Los Angeles. That was my only plan. I didn't know how to drive. I didn't have a place to stay, except with this guy for a while. And I didn't have any money to get a car or an apartment. So about thirty minutes into our cross-country drive, it started to seem like a crazy idea. But like my mom always taught me, I had to live with my choice.

From the time I left high school, I only wanted to act, but I had no idea what steps had to happen to make that a job. Nobody gave me any information on how to break through into a career, and I would just audition when parts were available.

When you're a teenager trying to figure it all out, you can fall into some things that you don't want as part of your life in the long run. Around age sixteen, I became dependent on drugs to make me feel good. It's no secret how that kind of shit ends.

By some sort of luck, I started hanging out at a youth center on Eighteenth Street. During the day, it was offices for drug rehab counselors. In the evening, it was a place where young people could come together and keep themselves from falling into bad things. I had already fallen in and out of bad things. But I'd show up and listen to people talking about why they did what they did and how they got free of it.

After a couple weeks, I started thinking to myself, *I don't want to do these drugs anymore either. I'd like to clean this up.*

I got into drug rehab and that got me into my first marriage. At age eighteen, I married my drug counselor. He was a great guy, and getting married made sense to me at the time, even though I remember my mom asking me, "Are you sure this is something you want to go through with?"

You know, I was young and I thought I was doing what was expected of me. Besides, I had already agreed to it. I didn't know what being in love should feel like. He seemed to be in love with me, so I didn't question it.

A year later my mom was dropping me off at the hospital to give birth to my daughter. In the '70s, you had to go into the delivery room on your own—just you, some nurses, and the doctor. These days, you can have a professional film crew in the room with you, led by a fucking marching band if you want it.

My mother told me, "Listen. You're going to be up there by yourself. If you need to cry out, then cry out."

So I thought that I was going to be okay. I knew it

was going to hurt. I'd grown up with really bad menstrual cramps, so I thought I was ready.

You can't possibly be ready for that kind of pain.

I made some noise. But then a nurse shut me down, saying, "Women do this every single day, all day long. What are you crying about?"

There's a reason I only gave birth once. That should tell you everything about the level of pain I experienced. You have no idea what labor is all about until you've done it yourself. They tell you it's a natural process. Nobody says, "Listen, this entails shoving a ninety-two-inch TV screen through a tiny hole. Good luck."

They say you forget the birth process in between having babies. Not a chance. That memory has stayed right with me.

I spent two days in the hospital afterward. There was no expectation of sympathy from the "What do you mean you don't feel good?" nursing staff. Every couple of hours, they would wheel Alex's bassinet in, and I was supposed to feed her. I did everything I could to get Alex to attach, but she was too busy looking around. She didn't want to latch on. Then the one time I got it to happen, she bit down on me and didn't let go.

That was it for me.

"Don't worry about it," Ma told me. "There's always formula."

A couple years into the marriage, I could tell that it wasn't for me. I liked my husband, but the "till death do us part" thing didn't seem like it would happen.

Also, I thought he understood that I would always want to act or perform. He didn't.

So I went back to my mom's house, and I told her, "I don't like being married."

She said, "Well, maybe it's because it wasn't something you wanted to really do. But you did it anyway."

I said, "Yeah. Maybe. Maybe." All the while knowing she was right.

She had asked me, "Are you sure?" long before we tied the knot. I thought it would be better if I did it my way. I loved my kid, but I didn't want to be only a wife and a mother.

When I told my mother that a couple of actors and I were driving across the country to California, she said, "You know, if you go and you don't like it, it's gonna be hard for me to get you back here because I don't have the money."

I was still thinking it would be better if I did it my way.

I said, "Well, let's see what happens."

I ended up in Lubbock, Texas, for two or three months while the two actors did a dinner theater show. Then after it ended, the one actor I knew best said we were heading to California next.

When we got there, I said to him, "Wait. This isn't LA."

And he said, "It's San Diego. This is where we're going to be."

I knew Hollywood. I knew Los Angeles. I had never heard of San Diego. But that was where I was going to live. My friend was associated with an upstart theater company called San Diego Repertory Theatre, which was in its first year. I fell in with that group, at first helping backstage and then getting cast in plays. It eventually became one of San Diego's premier theater companies with three stages and art galleries. In 1977, though, we did shows wherever space was available.

After a few months, I knew I didn't want to keep sharing a house with the actor. I kept my mother abreast of my situation but didn't say I had no idea how I was going to manage. I had to figure it out. All I knew was that I had a kid and you don't get to fall apart when you have a kid.

Some people I met in San Diego said, "Since you have a kid, you need to go on welfare."

I was appalled. I thought it was the worst idea. My mother had never ever taken assistance.

They encouraged me, "Things are different now. Listen, you need the money to take care of yourself and Alex and have some medical insurance. Besides, you paid into it with your other jobs."

I applied because I knew they were right. I ended up getting $127 a month and some food stamps. And that's how I figured it out. I had other small jobs on the side, but I had to be careful because whatever I made, they would take it out of the next welfare check.

My mom would ask, "How are you doing?"

I finally told her I was on welfare.

I knew my mother didn't like the idea of it. And I was feeling really, you know, dodgy about doing it.

Then my mother, in the same way she always did, said, "Stop thinking about what I'm thinking. It's what you have to do. You have a kid to take care of, so you will do what you need to do."

In those days you could rent a pretty great place for little money. And somebody recommended that I meet an interracial couple who lived near Balboa Park and had three small separate places on their property. They had twins who looked like Alex, and living close to each other would be a great situation for their kids and for Alex.

They rented one of the little houses to me. It was really nice, and it looked like a gorgeous tree house because it had two giant tree trunks coming through the deck. It was a tiny place, only a bedroom, a little front room, a bathroom, and a kitchen, but it was the first place I ever had to myself. I would sit with Alex out on the deck and feel like I was so lucky, mostly because folks extended themselves to help me out. I was offered a scholarship to learn cosmetology and how to do hair. And I managed to get myself a used moped and a driver's license, and I would take Alex off to preschool before I'd go to my hair-cutting classes.

I'd do hair by day and work with the San Diego Rep at night, and I figured out how to get by with some food stamps and about thirty welfare bucks a week.

Years later, my mother told me that she had felt concerned, but she said, "There was nothing I could do. I didn't have any money either. I had no way to rescue you. So, you know, I figured you would figure it out."

After I had made a couple of movies, I sent a check back to the state of California, repaying them for the welfare assistance they had given me. It got me through a rough time. It gets other folks through. It's needed.

Once I started getting parts in plays, I wanted a name that sounded more interesting. Caryn Johnson wasn't it. Some people at the Rep called me Whoopi because I would sometimes let loose with a fart. I added "Cushione" to it, with a French pronunciation. Then, I got a review written by journalist Welton Jones. It was a good one, so I sent it to my mother.

Later, when we talked on the phone, she said, "What is this Whoopi Cushione?"

"Well, it's kind of my nickname. It's like 'whoopee cushion' with a little French accent."

She said, "Well, I picked that up. But why? Why Whoopi?"

So, I explained to her the whole farting thing.

"Well, if you're going to change your name and want people to take you seriously, you need a more substantial name," my mother advised me.

I said, "Oh, really, great namer of the stars? What do you think it should be?"

She said, "Well, you should take one of the names from the family tree. How about Goldberg? That has a nice ring to it."

That became my name. Only my family and a few people who knew me early in my life still called me Caryn.

Through the San Diego Rep, I met a very creative

guy, Dave, who had come down from Berkeley to do a show. He was a member of an avant-garde theater group called the Blake Street Hawkeyes, and he thought I should move north and act with them.

For a woman who wanted to get to Los Angeles, it still wasn't happening. I went from San Diego, bypassed LA, and went straight to the San Francisco area. I left San Diego as Caryn Johnson and arrived in Berkeley as Whoopi Goldberg. I really dug Dave. He was cool with helping parent my kid and she liked him, so we got together as a couple.

At the Blake Street theater, I was around creative people who gave me stage time and a chance to improvise and develop some characters. I had about eleven or twelve characters that I had come up with. I started performing, building various characters, trying them out on stage. After a while, I had enough material to do a solo show. I called it *The Spook Show* because the audience would never know which characters might appear in a show. People started showing up to see me on stage, and I was having a good time. Dave also had a solo show, and we even took off to do them in Europe for a couple months.

After all was said and done, things started to happen for me. One night Alice Walker, the Pulitzer Prize–winning writer of *The Color Purple*, came to see the show.

I met her afterward when she came backstage. She told me that they were thinking about turning her book into a movie.

I said to her, "I know I'm here doing my thing, but if they do that, I'd play the washbowl on the counter. I'd play the dirt on the doormat. You name it. I'd love to be part of it."

The National Endowment for the Arts was becoming more supportive of experimental stuff, and soon I got a letter from the artistic director of the Dance Theater Workshop in New York, David White. He wrote that they were doing a series of one-person shows. He had my show highly recommended to him by a colleague who saw it, and so he was inviting me to do it in New York during their series. He said there was an itty-bitty stipend for me, but that I'd have to figure out where I could stay. He wanted to know if I would be interested in doing the series.

I called him up. "Listen, your theater is on Seventeenth Street. I grew up on Twenty-Sixth and Tenth. Hell yeah, I'll be there."

I talked to my mom. "I'm coming to New York because these guys at the Dance Theater Workshop want me to do shows there, stuff that I've written for myself in the last couple years."

She was happy about it. I had not seen my mom face-to-face in about four years. I stayed with her in my old apartment in the projects. She was finishing up her master's degree and teaching full-time at the Head Start preschool.

She said, "Do you mind if I come with you to the shows?"

I told her, "I'm just gonna let you know, I don't know what to expect."

Like I thought, for the first week of the show, only about six or seven people came. My mom would scan the audience and report to me if she saw someone she recognized. Little by little, more people came.

One night, when the audience only had twenty people, my mother told me, "Oh, my God. *One Potato, Two Potato* Barbara Barrie is here."

Most people know her as the wife on the TV show *Barney Miller*. She's an incredible stage and film actress and was the white lead in *One Potato, Two Potato*, a 1964 film that featured her in a relationship with a black man, played by Bernie Hamilton. It was a big deal, especially in 1964.

Then, about a week later, there was a review in the *New York Times* by Mel Gussow that changed the course of my whole life. He liked the show. A lot.

Suddenly, the seats were filling up. You couldn't get a ticket.

Burt Bacharach, the big-time composer of hits like "I'll Never Fall in Love Again" and "Walk on By," came in to see the show one night. Designer Norma Kamali was there another night. Every night there was another famous face that my mother recognized: Anne Meara, Jerry Stiller, Bette Midler, and even Oscar Hammerstein's wife.

One night before the show, my mother came backstage and said, "I just want to tell you something, but I don't want you to get overexcited or nervous."

I said, "You're making me nervous. What's happening?"

"I just want you to know that Mike Nichols is in the audience."

"You mean like *The Graduate* Mike Nichols?"

"Yes. He's directing two shows on Broadway now. *The Real Thing*, a Tom Stoppard play with Glenn Close and Jeremy Irons, and he's doing *Hurlyburly*."

I went out on stage, and I did my show. I didn't know what Mike Nichols looked like, so I just did what I do and didn't think about it.

At the end of the show, I went back to my dressing room and sat down. My mother said, "Did you see him?"

Right then, there was a knock on the dressing room door.

My mother went to answer the door, and she said, "Mike Nichols is here."

I went to meet him, and he was standing there with tears in his eyes.

The first character I did in the show was a drug addict named Fontaine who goes to Amsterdam. He sees Anne Frank's hiding place and her quote about how she believed in the goodness of people despite everything. He sees Shelley Winters's Oscar that she donated to the museum. It all becomes very real to Fontaine, and it changes him.

That piece of the show really got to Mike.

"I don't know how to explain this to you," he said. "But I was on the last boat leaving Germany in 1939 before they no longer allowed Jews to leave."

Quite a few characters in the show tore Mike up, like the thirteen-year-old who has to do a coat hanger abortion on herself after her family kicks her out, and the disabled woman, trapped in a wheelchair, who sleeps and dreams she is a dancer.

Judith Ivey, the actress currently starring in one of the plays Mike was directing, *Hurlyburly*, had brought him to see the show. He had no idea what to expect. There was a lot going on in the show that he loved.

He said, "Could we have a conversation soon?"

I said, "Of course. Sure."

"Would you ever consider doing your show on Broadway?"

I said, "Yes. Of course I would."

I looked over at my mother, and she was sitting there, all poised, listening to Mike talk, rather blasé, as if this was something that happened around her every single day.

Mike got up to leave, saying, "Let me have your phone number. I'll have to figure out how to do this and I'll call you." He hugged me and then turned and gave my mom a hug.

My mother closed the door behind him, and we both screamed silently because we knew Mike was still nearby.

A couple weeks later, I wrapped up the show. My mother and I had a great time together, laughing a lot. I told her I loved her and flew back to Berkeley.

About a month later, I was home cleaning up the kitchen when the phone rang. "Ms. Goldberg, this is Mike Nichols."

I said, "Yeah, I recognize the voice."

"Well, I found the theater," he said. "And my partner and I would like to bring you to New York."

"Seriously? Really?"

"Yes. You sound surprised."

"Yeah, I'm surprised because I thought you were kidding. I didn't think you were actually going to do it."

He said, "No. I wasn't kidding and we are going to do it."

About five months went by, and then I went back to New York to rehearse for *Whoopi Goldberg* at the Lyceum Theatre. Mike got an apartment for me to live in while I was doing the show, a really cool old brownstone. So I had my mom move in with me since Alex was staying in Berkeley with Dave so she wouldn't miss out on regular grammar school.

Mike and I went to rehearsals together, and my mom would come and sit near Mike. He really liked my mom, and they had a great time together, talking, laughing, and smoking cigarettes. To me, they were very much alike. I never told Mike about what had happened to my mother and her hospitalization. They'd both been kids who had nothing, who had to look to find their place in the world, and then, you know, became the people they were meant to become. Both were self-made people.

We had been rehearsing for about a week in a Broadway theater, and one afternoon I was doing my thing on stage. And Mike started to shift in his chair.

"Can I stop you?"

I said, "Yeah."

And he said, with a big, deep sigh, "Does this story have an end?"

"Yeah, yeah, it does."

"I'm so glad you know that. Because you came to the end of the story quite a while ago."

"You're right," I said. "I'm not listening to myself because I've done this a lot. I know it all so well."

Mike came to the edge of the stage. "You can't be on automatic like that. You have to keep yourself ready for anything that happens because you're an improviser. There's no reason to let it get old. You don't have to nail your own feet to the floor like that."

I apologized and admitted that I was bored with the performance.

He said, "If you're bored, do something about it. Think about it. You have to pay attention to what you're doing. Because if you're not paying attention, I'm not going to pay attention."

He started calling out topics, and I'd have the character shift and start off in a different direction, talking on the topic. Then Mike would say something else, and I'd switch and have the character follow whatever he was talking about. It was great for me because it kept me present.

After that, over the course of a couple of days, we had a great time, and the show got better and better. Mike gave me permission to fly on stage.

Even off the stage, Mike always let me feel like I belonged where I was. Not like a newcomer. He always invited me along to whatever he had going on. If my mom was there, he included her.

One day Mike said, "Come with me. I'm having lunch with Carl, Paul, and Steve."

I said, "Okay. Will they mind if I go?"

He shrugged it off. "No, no, no. They won't mind."

I was thinking about how I was being invited to meet his friends. I mean, I know people named Carl, Paul, and Steve, too. Regular folks.

I headed over to this lunch place to meet up with Mike, and he waved me over to his table, where he was sitting with Carl Reiner, Paul Simon, and Steve Martin. He introduced me, even though I knew exactly who they were.

I kept telling myself, *Okay. Just keep breathing. Breathe.* It was pretty amazing.

And that wasn't the last lunch or dinner with show business greats. I got to meet other actors, directors, and producers at the very beginning of my career that I would have never met on my own, all because of Mike.

The best part, for me, was taking my mom along on these lunches. Mike would treat my mom like she was a queen who had graced us all at the table. Even though she was shy, she loved meeting these people we had watched or listened to for years and years.

The day before my show opened on Broadway, I was walking down Seventh Avenue with Nan Leonard, a publicist working on promoting the show. We were talking, and she stopped me.

"I want you to just savor this moment," she said.

"Being on Broadway, you mean?" I asked her.

"No," she said. "Savor the fact that nobody knows who you are right now. Because after today, that's all going to be different. That's going to change."

I thought she was, you know, waxing on.

She said, "Soon, even truck drivers are going to know Whoopi Goldberg. People will recognize you."

I didn't believe it could happen. But she was right. What she told me came true.

Chapter Eleven

When Mike Nichols put his name to something, lots of folks would show up to see what it was about.

Mike knew all about performing. He had been on the stage as an improviser and actor for years. When he was starting out, his Broadway show with Elaine May was a big hit. After that, he proved that he was very skilled at directing for stage and film. Everybody knew Mike Nichols's name. And before Mike Nichols chose me, very few people knew my name. So, count me lucky from the get-go.

About a week or so before my show opened, I came in to rehearse and saw a small white-haired man and his tiny well-dressed wife sitting with Mike. They looked like Mr. and Mrs. Santa Claus.

Mike didn't introduce me like he usually did. He

only said, "Okay, let's get through some of the pieces you want to hit. Let me take a look."

So, I just went on doing my thing on stage. I didn't give it much thought. The couple was laughing and having a good time.

Then opening night rolled around. My mom went with me to my dressing room, and it was completely full with tons of crazy stuff—opening night presents, lots of flower arrangements, and notes on every countertop like you see in the movies.

My mother started reading the cards on the flower arrangements. Famous people I had never met had sent me their "break a leg" wishes. It was amazing.

"These flowers are from Diana Ross," my mother said, pointing out a big vase of roses.

I said, "I don't know Diana Ross, but that's really great."

"Well, she knows who you are."

I was overwhelmed by the support.

Against the wall of my dressing room were two wrapped packages, leaning up against the wall.

I opened the first one: a framed Hirschfeld drawing of me in poses of each of my characters. The little Santa Claus man at rehearsal that day had been Al Hirschfeld, who was there to draw my caricature. If you know about him, he began to hide his daughter's name, Nina, in his drawings after she was born in 1945. Next to his signature he would write the number of times he had hidden her name in his art. In mine he put Nina's name forty times, the most of any drawing he had ever done. I was blown away.

The second wrapped present was a huge surprise. It was from Mike and my mother. At some point during rehearsal, Mike and I had talked about the actor Sam Waterston, who starred in the stage version of *Hamlet* in New York. I had seen him in various productions when I was younger, and I told Mike what a great actor he is and that I loved watching him do his thing. I am a big admirer of Sam's incredible talent.

I pulled the paper away from the gift to find a giant framed poster of Sam Waterston as Hamlet, signed by Sam to me.

Mike understood me. He understood my mom a lot. I don't know why. He just did.

After the show was an opening night party. I wasn't familiar with the traditions on Broadway, and, I have to say, it was something to be feted by all those well-known people. Jack Nicholson, Calvin Klein, and Liza Minnelli attended.

At one point Paul Simon grabbed my mom and said,

"You have to make sure she enjoys this. When it all happened for Artie and me, we didn't know we were supposed to enjoy it. We didn't. I hope she understands that, regardless of what people say to her, she's got to enjoy it now because this part only happens once."

My mom passed the message along to me right away. I heard it. I enjoyed myself and soaked it all in.

Ruth Gordon and her husband, Garson Kanin, came to see my show. I have been a big fan of both since I was a kid. I always knew who they were. They said, "You have to let us take you to lunch."

I thought, *Hell yeah. I'm gonna let Minnie Castevet from* Rosemary's Baby, *one of the best horror films of all time, take me to lunch.* Her husband had written *Born Yesterday*, which my mom and I had watched whenever it was on TV. *Yeah, I'm definitely going to lunch with them.*

After that opening night and for the whole run of the 156 shows, my mother and I and almost any celebrity you can name would often go to lunch or dinner somewhere. Almost better to me than getting to meet these famous folks myself was seeing my mother get to meet them. Watching her share a meal with these famous actors, performers, and directors she had watched for years was amazing. For me, whatever my mom wanted to do, that's what I wanted to do. I wanted better things for her than for me. I wanted to make sure that what-ever it was, she was going to be part of it. I wanted her to have great times for all the Coney Island days and for taking us to see the Rockettes, the Ice Capades, the circus, the museums, the Beatles, and all the other days she made magnificence happen. For all the ways she had enriched my childhood and my imagination, I wanted this as a way to thank her.

Just like the publicist had told me, folks started to recognize me on the street. Sometimes, that worked out really well. Often the traffic in Manhattan to the Broad-way district was really thick, and even catching a cab to get to the theater and get ready on time could be risky. Quite a few times, one of the horse-drawn carriage driv-ers would recognize me and pick up my mom and me on their way to Central Park and drop us at the theater.

Everything started to move forward pretty fast. Sandy Gallin, a huge entertainment manager, took me on as a client. I got an agent. A whole new time in my life was opening up.

Because of Mike Nichols, I got the attention of Steven Spielberg. He was going to direct the movie adap-tation of *The Color Purple*, and he wanted me to audition for the lead role of Celie. That started up a long audition process that took almost a year. The cast was huge, and he had a lot to do, figuring out what it would all look like. At that time, I didn't know that he was pretty set on me playing Celie.

I knew I wouldn't be going back to being onstage with the Blake Street Hawkeyes, and Dave knew it, too. Even though he was the first one to say "go for it" when I got the Broadway offer, he didn't want to be on standby, waiting to see what would happen between us. He told me he'd take care of Alex until I could figure it out, but he was ready to move on and not have the responsibility.

I had saved up a lot of my Broadway money, and I really wanted to keep my mom around me. She was my best check-in. She kept it all real for me. I also needed help looking after Alex. Mom was still teaching preschool and was living back in our apartment in the projects. I didn't know what she would want to do. She had worked hard to get her master's degree, and I didn't know if she would want to leave her place in Head Start behind. But I thought I'd ask.

I called her from California with my proposition. "Ma, would you ever consider coming to California? I'm going back and forth to LA and New York to audition, and Alex is in school, so I need some help."

She didn't hesitate for long. "Yes. When do you want me there?"

"I got to tell you, Ma. It may be a while you'll be here."

"I don't have a problem with that."

"Great. Great. I can buy you a plane ticket as soon as you can come," I told her.

I went to pick her up at the airport after a few weeks had gone by, and she walked off the plane carrying two brown shopping bags.

"What's in the bags?" I asked her.

"Everything I wanted to take."

"So, where are your suitcases?"

"This is it," she said. "This much is what I brought."

"But did you close up the apartment? What will happen with that?"

She stopped walking and faced me. "Listen. I left everything. I took what I wanted. I dropped the house key into the incinerator, and I left."

"Wait! You did what?"

She repeated, "I dropped the key into the incinerator and left for the airport."

I still couldn't grasp it. "Well, what about all the stuff still in the house? What about your books, the Beatles albums, and everything else?"

"I'm looking at this as a fresh start," she told me. "There's no point in bringing all that with me. Besides, you didn't ever say that I should save you the albums or anything in that apartment, did you?"

She was right about that, so I couldn't say more. "Okay, I get it. But . . . what about stuff like our birth certificates?"

Ma got in the front seat of my Volkswagen Bug. "You can always get another one."

I still couldn't quite understand what she was telling me. "Ma, what happened to—"

She stopped me in the middle. "Caryn, I don't know what you want me to say. I brought what I wanted, and I didn't want to bring the rest. I can get what I need here in California. I didn't want to bring that old life into this new one."

That was it. That's all there was to be said about it. She never returned to the projects, and I have no idea where anything from our old apartment went. I'm sure somebody scored some cash on those first-run Beatles albums. I keep waiting for my birth certificate to pop up in a tabloid magazine one day, but it never has.

Years and years later, after she had told me the secret about her memory loss after Bellevue, it made sense. The move to California was probably the first time she had felt safe, like nobody was going to show up and take her back to Bellevue. I got it. She wanted to be free. It became clear to me.

I knew I had a goal. From then on, I felt like my life's calling was to take the load off my mom, to give her a good time. She had carried it long enough.

My mother was the first person I told when I was offered the part of Celie, months before the cast was public.

"So, you're going to be in a Steven Spielberg movie," my mother said. And then we did a jig in celebration.

I was going to be the only major cast member who had never been in a film or a TV show before. Even though I wanted the part, I felt the pressure of Spielberg taking a risk on me.

After I got the final word, I said to Steven, "What if I suck?"

He said, "You've sucked before, haven't you?"

"Well, yeah."

"Okay, you'll just suck again. I'll do my best to keep that from happening. You've sucked before, but you didn't suck every day, right?"

"Yeah, okay."

"So, there might be times when you suck—it's true for everybody. But I still believe you can and should play this part."

It took me a while to get used to filming instead of

theater. I didn't know that films are not shot in the order of how the story goes, the way a play happens. It's too expensive. So they have to film all the scenes that take place in a certain location all together. Like every scene inside the speakeasy was shot, and then we'd move on to a different location.

I was not used to not having a live audience and having to do repeated takes of the same scene so the cameras could catch it from every angle.

Early in the shooting, I asked Steven, "How do you know if somebody's laughing? How do you know if you got it without the audience reacting to you?"

He called me over to stand next to him in front of the camera. He pointed into the lens. "Look in there. That's where all those people are. Right down there. You won't be able to hear them. Because if you could hear them, we wouldn't be able to do the takes. So, you have to know that they are laughing or crying silently."

The other thing he told me was, "If you're really present in the scene, you can see and feel it in your crew. The crew knows more about good acting and making movies than you will ever know, so treat them like platinum."

He taught me to respect what the crew needed from me, to trust them. If they say they need something from you, go with it. If you treat your crew poorly, it's not going to go well for you. I thank God that Steven trained me that way from the very beginning. My career work ethic has always been this: take care of the crew.

I would call my mom every day at the end of filming, and we'd laugh and talk, and I'd tell her the secrets of filmmaking that no one else sees when they're watching a movie.

"Ma, there's going to be a scene where I'm running to my sister in a field full of sunflowers. Well, there really isn't a field. They brought in hundreds of buckets full of sunflower plants and lined them all up to look like a field."

She loved hearing about it all.

"How do they make those rooms look so full of cigarette and cigar smoke?" she asked me.

"It's a machine with dry ice and some ingredient that makes smoke, and they blow that across the set before shooting the scene."

Every day I'd call her and give her some new insight, except when I tried to tell her how they made it look like someone was bleeding.

"No, that can't be fake. I'm going to still believe it's real blood," Ma said.

When I got my first Oscar nomination for *The Color Purple*, I didn't know how I felt about it. I knew I was

good in the movie and that it was worthy of a nomination, but I didn't expect one.

The day it was announced, my mother and I laughed
and giggled all morning because we were both Oscars
fanatics. We had never missed watching one. As a kid,
I had written hundreds of acceptance speeches for when
I won my own Oscar. But when it really happened,
I thought, *How will I actually get up and give a speech if
I do win?*

People kept calling me all day, telling me I was going
to win.

I said to my mother, "This is all just very odd. I don't
know how to feel about any of this."

And she said, "Well, the first thing you should
remind yourself of is that you may not win. I know
people are already saying to you that you're gonna get
it. That may not happen. You may not. So you need to
just be glad you got here, the first time out."

I knew she was right. I was looking at the other
women up for Best Actress: Anne Bancroft, Jessica
Lange, Meryl Streep, and Geraldine Page, all my favorites, every single one of them.

Geraldine Page and her husband, Rip Torn, lived
in Chelsea when I was kid, and we would see them out
and about in the neighborhood. Everybody knew who

they were because they did Broadway shows. I never had the money to see her when I was a kid, but I'd read about her shows in the newspaper. I also knew she had been nominated for an Oscar many times and had never won one. To me, she is one of those be-all and end-all actors. Same with Anne Bancroft. They were both very New York, but they also were in many films. That's how I knew their acting work. I was like, *Oh, my God, here I am in their company.*

After the nominations were announced, some people made little digs aimed at me. People in the press were trying to make me feel bad because I was nominated for my very first movie, with a "how dare you" attitude. Then, I began thinking, *Fuck you. I was nominated because they thought I was good enough. And I don't care what any of you boneheads say.*

So, the night arrived, and I was sitting in a gown in the audience of the Academy Awards. I saw Jack Nicholson, Don Ameche, Anjelica Houston, and Harrison Ford all sitting close by. I was thinking about how Ma would have liked seeing Harrison Ford in person. She was a big fan of his. She called Harrison Ford and Tom Cruise "journeyman actors." They rarely get nominated, but they are the actors the whole movie depends on. Those were always her favorites, those unsung hardworking actors that carry the whole plotline.

When my category came up, the presenter was F. Murray Abraham, who had won an Oscar the year before for playing Salieri in *Amadeus*. He read the names of each of the nominees, and then he opened the envelope and paused. He said how he had revered the winner for decades. I knew it was Geraldine Page for her performance in *A Trip to Bountiful*. And I was thinking, *You're not the only one who feels that way about her.*

He announced Geraldine's name. I was applauding like crazy. As she was walking to the stage, the actor sitting next to me said, "Why did you applaud so much when she beat you?"

I said, "What do you mean? That's Geraldine Page. You know, she's Geraldine Page." I gave a quick list of everything she had been in. This was her win, and in a way mine too because I was also a New York actor. I was thinking, *She's a New York actor. I'm a New York actor.* And that was good enough for me.

The next year she passed away. So, yeah, I was happy it happened for her that year.

Even though I didn't win, between doing the Broadway show with Mike Nichols and *The Color Purple* with Steven Spielberg, I knew I had something. I thought

I was talented. I will tell you that people don't want you to get too excited about yourself. Between growing up with my mother telling me that I could do whatever I wanted to do, and Mike Nichols and Steven Spielberg reiterating that to me with their belief, I felt like I could walk up to people, look them in the eye, and say, "Yeah, I can do that part."

They walked me in the door. They said, "We're vouching for her. We're walking her in because she has talent." I got my confidence because they knew what I was capable of doing. I would call Mike if I was in doubt about what I could do—he always had me in his sights. I stopped listening to other people who gave me a list of reasons why I couldn't do certain roles. I knew those people didn't know anything about me or what I might be capable of. Even after Broadway and my first feature film, I still wanted the opportunity to do what I believed I could do.

About two weeks before Mike Nichols passed away, Cynthia Nixon called me to say Mike wanted her and me and Christine Baranski to meet him for lunch. We all had a two-hour lunch. We laughed and told stories and listened to Mike tell stories. I knew that this man's effect on me and my luck with him coming to my show all those years ago put me in wondrous company. It seemed like Mike was thinner and didn't have the energy he once had. We all figured he was eighty-three now, so none of us mentioned it to each other. I didn't know it would be my last time seeing him. None of us did.

When he died of a heart attack in November 2014, I had just dealt with my brother's death in May. The people I loved the most in the world just seemed to keep leaving . . . were no longer in the world.

I was supposed to talk about the loss of Mike on *The View* the next day, but I couldn't. I couldn't stop crying long enough to say anything. Many of us gathered at his home, and Mary-Louise Parker and I were bartering with God. We wanted Mike back—was there anyone we could offer God instead? Had we not been so crushed, I bet we could have figured something out.

Mike Nichols's friendship and belief in me still sustain me.

Chapter Twelve

I knew that my daughter was going to be really angry at me, and maybe for a long time. Kids want their moms. They want their moms to be around to take care of everything they don't know how to handle yet. They want their moms' full attention whenever they need it. They want their moms to be home when they go to bed and be there when they wake up. That's how it goes. Kids want their moms to think about them first, not the next offer on the career table.

As an adult, Alex remembers me explaining to her, as a child, why I often had to be away. She gets it now. But as a kid, you're not thinking about financial independence, security, or having some backup in the bank account. When you're eight or nine, you just want your mom around.

Years later, it occurred to me that I had kind of done to Alex what had happened to me in my childhood when my mom was hospitalized. There were some differences. I couldn't talk to my mom and had no idea when or if I'd ever see her again. Alex could always call me and find me. I never knew which adult might be in our house when I got home from school. Alex had my mom with her morning, noon, and night.

Here's the deal. A regular mom might have said something like, "Yeah, I'd like to play a role in your movie or do my solo show in Vegas or have a TV series, but I'm a mom. In ten or twelve years, when my kid is grown, I'll check back in with you."

It doesn't happen like that. I knew my opportunities wouldn't hang around and wait on me. I knew they wouldn't come my way ever again.

In the larger view, what I wanted most was to be a "genie in a bottle" for my mom, my brother, and my kid. I wanted to give my mom a chance to live with a whole lot less worry. I wanted my brother to be with us and enjoy his life, too. I wanted Alex to have the ability to do more, live in a good house with her own bedroom, and have more options than we had before Broadway came calling for me.

I'd say to Alex, "Do you remember when you were

six and I could only get you one pair of shoes? And now you have seven or eight pairs. You have the toys you want and we get to go to Disneyland and other stuff you like a lot."

I knew that didn't make it okay in her mind because little kids don't think about what it takes to make money, but it mattered to me. I didn't want to let the chance to upgrade our lives pass by. So, I asked the best person in the world to help me raise my kid, my own mother. I knew Alex was always safe and loved and heard. And I took the opportunities as they came while I was still in the circle of actors with that kind of attention. I already knew that post-Oscar-nomination buzz doesn't last long in Hollywood. At the same time, I still understood that kids want their own mom.

My mom got it. She told me, "You go do what you need to do. I'm here with Alex. I've got this."

So, my mom, once again, made it all possible for me.

I was able to look into lots of opportunities being handed to me right and left. As soon as Oscar night for *The Color Purple* was over, I started hearing people, at all levels in film, saying things like, "Well, you know, you are black. So, there's not a lot of stuff producers are going to hire you for."

Or I'd go to a studio to read for a movie, and they'd say, "Well, you're not exactly what we were looking for."

I don't think I really understood for a long time what that actually meant, and I really thought that if I got a part, that might change minds. I once told someone that I wanted to play Eleanor of Aquitaine, one of the greatest parts ever written for an actor, because that's what actors do. Another time I said I would have loved to play the Princess Bride, another great part for an actor. People started explaining that the whole black thing could be a problem if those were the kinds of parts I thought I would be going after. I said, "But that's what actors do . . . right?" I knew I was black, had been black my whole life, but people kept mentioning it like they were surprised.

Producers, agents, and directors would try to break it down to their reasons. "Well, visually, the viewers or audience has to believe that you can do what you're doing on-screen or on the stage."

I'd say, "But people go through stuff all the time. Black people do, too. It wasn't like I woke up as somebody else and then said, 'Oh, I think I will go back to being black now.' I've been black the whole time. So I feel like you're trying to tell me that black people could not, or did not, or cannot possibly go through this experience, because I'm telling you, I know all about this. That's just not true."

They weren't writing major movies for black people in the 1980s either. That's why Spielberg taking a chance on *The Color Purple* was a big deal. You know, before my nomination in 1985, there were only fifteen black nominees in the history of the Academy Awards, and only three black winners: Hattie McDaniel, Sidney Poitier, and Lou Gossett Jr. That's it. And that didn't bother a whole lot of folks in Hollywood.

One day I was sitting next to my mother at an event, and she leaned over and said, "How can they not know that you can do anything? How can they doubt what you are able to do after they look at what you've done already?"

She got that I was feeling panicked about the future. I knew I was lucky to have started out with a role as good as Celie in *The Color Purple*. It was clear that parts for black actors weren't coming up and available twice a year. But being in a Spielberg movie and working with Mike Nichols made me believe that I could play any role, whatever was up. I knew I could. It didn't matter if they wanted me to play a monkey or a monster. It didn't matter if they wanted me to play a white lady, a black lady, a yellow or brown lady. I could do them all. So, I was boisterous about that. I spoke up for myself.

Most of the movie roles I played in the '80s and '90s were intended for other people. My lead role in *Burglar* in 1987 was supposed to be for Bruce Willis. I was being considered for a supporting role as his neighbor. When he turned the lead down, I asked, "How about me?" It took a while for the producers to believe in me.

Jumpin' Jack Flash was written for *Cheers* sitcom star Shelley Long. It was Penny Marshall's first directing gig. Not sure what happened with Shelley, but I had a really good time playing that part. I wish people had shown up at the movie theater for it.

Lots of folks tell me they loved that movie, but they saw it years later when it was released for television.

I was never the first choice for the role of Rita, the tough narcotics officer in *Fatal Beauty*. That role was written specifically for Cher. And *Sister Act* was supposed to be for Bette Midler.

Some of the movies were good, some were okay, and some flatlined altogether.

I started hearing the press say stuff like, "She's not living up to her Oscar potential." People seemed to feel that I was disappointing them.

And for about ten minutes, I took it to heart.

I asked my mother, "Are you unhappy with me?"

She said, "In what way?"

"Well, do you think I'm making bad choices in my movies?"

She didn't hesitate at all. "Caryn, you are making the choices you make. Have you had a good time making the movies you made?"

"Yeah, I have. But they haven't made much money for the studios."

She said, "If it's about the money, then, you know, you probably will disappoint people all the time because you can't always get those films like *Color Purple*. Nobody does."

She saw where I was coming from. She told me, "You're a working actor; I don't see where that's an issue. Because you're a character actor working as a lead actor."

Mike Nichols said the same thing to me. "Listen, you're working as an actor. Making money for them is great, but there's no guarantee. There's no guarantee ever about what a movie is going to do. You never know. So it's not up to you."

During the '80s, I was making some other types of choices, and I knew they weren't good. I kept those to myself or hid them, for the most part. I had stayed pretty far away from drugs, except for pot, after getting cleaned up in the early '70s. But Los Angeles and New York started to redefine what "recreational drug use" meant in the '80s. I was invited to parties where I was greeted at the door with a bowl of Quaaludes from which I could pick what I wanted. Lines of cocaine were laid across tables and bathroom counters for the taking. Everybody knew the cops weren't going to raid the Beverly Hills, Bel Air, or Hollywood Hills house of a big-time producer or actor, so the attitude was very relaxed. Everyone partook. You knew you were going to get high for a couple hours and then get laid before the night was over.

Since my previous problem had been other kinds of drugs, I thought I could handle the cocaine thing. It didn't seem dangerous. Everybody seemed to have access to it, even on TV and movie sets. The cops were never going to raid a studio either.

It was a really good time for about a year. Then I fell into the deep well of cocaine and sank to a new low. Nobody around me caught on to where I was at with it. At least, that's what I wanted to believe. I would have called myself "a very high-functioning addict." I'd still show up on the set on time, do my job, and keep pace with the production. I knew people wouldn't get a paycheck if I didn't show up. Whatever had to happen, I could still make it happen.

Then cocaine started to kick my ass. I'd go to work and realize I was getting sloppy. I didn't like it. I knew it wasn't good. At one point, I hallucinated that something was under my bed and I'd be attacked if I got up. So I didn't move out of bed for twenty-four hours. That kind of shit doesn't end pretty. There's only so long a person can hold their bladder.

Finally, I had one of those slap-in-the-face moments that make you see pretty fucking clearly that you've hit bottom. I was staying in a very upscale hotel in Manhattan for my birthday. Somebody had given me an ounce of cocaine. I was sitting on the closet floor, just putting it up my nose. All by myself. I didn't hear the housekeeper knock or let herself in the room to clean it up.

She opened the closet door.

I screamed.

She screamed and backed up and looked like she was going to run.

I had to get to her quickly and try to calm her down. She was staring at my face as I talked. Once she understood it was my room, she calmed down and left. I looked at myself in the mirror near the door and saw cocaine all over my face.

I'd have been so embarrassed if my mother knew the extent the coke had me in its clutches. It's not like she didn't have recreational habits that she enjoyed. She was a smoker most of her life and wasn't at all opposed to smoking some weed, or even growing some between her rosebushes in the backyard in Berkeley.

But what I was doing was different. I was letting something else run my life and take me over. I didn't need my mom to be disappointed or pissed at me— I was pissed enough at myself. *Is this the version of yourself you're okay showing your daughter? WTF are you doing? Get up, get out, and fix your life. You've been sitting in a closet for two days. It's not good. Not good at all.*

Again, I am the luckiest woman in the world. I was able to stop using drugs quickly. Not everyone can. I certainly know a lot of people who have different brains, and they can't decide to quit. It's not a choice for them.

I accepted that I was probably going to gain weight and it wasn't going to be easy for a long time. I knew I'd have to change out my friends and turn down invitations, but I could do that. I didn't want to die. And I didn't want my kid to think her mom was an addict. I didn't want my mom to think her daughter was an addict. So, I got myself as straight as an arrow—an arrow that gained twenty pounds in the next year. I thought, *Okay, this is the exchange. This is what it's going to look like. If you want to stay alive, you gotta be okay with this.*

I had already decided that I was willing and ready to stop, so I was going to do whatever I needed to stop putting drugs up my nose. Just like the confines of the projects weren't going to be the confines of my future, neither was doing drugs.

My mom's lifelong belief in me turned into my mantra: "I can do anything I want if I put my mind to it." I mostly applied it to my flexibility as an actor, but it also kept me going so that I could have this career I had always wanted since I could speak.

Because the cast of *The Color Purple* was primarily black actors, the crew knew how to work with us, from the lighting to the makeup to the hair. When I started making movies after that, I had to give people time to get used to me. I asked a million questions. I stayed on the set because there's nothing better than watching the how-to of movie making. Everyone has their job. I loved being part of it. But I didn't see a lot of people of color, nor did I see a lot of women.

People would continue to say things to me like, "Oh, you're so articulate," as if that was a pleasant surprise. Or the producers or stylists would look at my hair, which I had been wearing in dreads since the late '70s, and say, "What are we supposed to do with this shit?"

I guess that every black actress they had worked with before me had either straightened her hair or worn it very short or worn a wig because that's what made the film people comfortable. I wasn't about to change my hair. Even my mom wore her hair in short locs after moving to California. We'd both rather read a book or watch a movie than pull a hot comb through our hair.

I finally said to my friend Julia Walker, who became my hair stylist on many of my films, "What don't they get? Why are they saying these stupid things to me?"

And Julia said, "They don't know any better. They don't know anyone like you. So to them, you are this kind of unicorn, somebody they've never come across. You don't quiet your mouth when you have something to say. I think you are very hard for them to understand. They thought you should be a lot easier to deal with than you are."

I came to understand that Julia was also a first for many people because she was a black woman who could do any actor's hair. Rarely did they ever let her, though. The stylist was usually someone white who was limited in what they could do because they couldn't do black hair. Often folks would say they could, but as soon as they started to spray your hair with water, you knew it was game over and that you would have to make a stink. And I did.

"I am easy to deal with, and I try to be polite," I told Julia, "unless they say or do something stupid like that."

"Well, that's the point. They don't know they're saying something stupid. But by the time it filters to your ear, you're like, 'That is the stupidest thing I've ever heard. And here's why.'"

Julia would tell me to adjust my attitude and not to give it so much attention by getting pissed about it. "They can't really get to you because you're the talent," she continued. "They can't question your right to be where you are. Instead, they'll just fuck with you in a way that they think will make you uncomfortable."

"I'm not uncomfortable. It's just stupid."

"They aren't thinking about how you're from New York and how all of those things don't matter to you." My makeup man, who came from makeup royalty, was Mike Germain, and he agreed with Julia. We spent many great years together, and I watched the two of them teach an industry that really didn't have much of a clue about black skin or hair to help move the needle forward. This was in the 1980s and 1990s, a long time ago, it seems, but Julia was right about a few things in all of this. Did they really think I would freak out because they were talking like that? There was nothing anyone could do to me or say about me that hadn't been done or said already.

There were times when I should have freaked out. Sometimes race was not the issue; sometimes it was something else. When I first heard about the movie *Ghost*, apparently every actress of color had auditioned for it.

I called my agent, Ron Meyer, and said, "Can I get an audition for this?"

My agent told me that they weren't going to consider me for the role of Oda Mae, the psychic medium scammer, because I was "too well known."

I said, "But every black woman, alive or dead, has auditioned for this."

He said, "I know, and we called about it, and they don't want you."

Patrick Swayze read the script and got the part of Sam, and he asked if I had turned the role of Oda Mae down. Bonnie Timmermann, the casting director, told him, "I've been pushing for her, but the writer doesn't feel she is right for it."

I don't know what Patrick said, but the next thing I knew, Ron called me in Alabama, where I was shooting another movie. He said to me, "Remember that part you wanted to read for? The director and lead actor want to come down to where you are and see if there is any chemistry between you and the lead actor."

And I said, "Who's that going to be?"

"Well, they said Patrick."

So I knew one of my favorite actors was coming to
see me in 'Bama, which is exactly what happened, and
the rest is history. Once he had the part, Patrick became
my advocate to play the role of Oda Mae. It was a big
deal for me that they came to Alabama, and it turned
out that Patrick and I had a really good connection in
the scenes. We had fun together. There was an energy
zapping back and forth between us. It was impossible
to ignore that it worked. I think Jerry Zucker still might
have had to convince some people, but between Bonnie
and Patrick and Jerry wanting me, I got the job. Jerry
said I could bring my best, and he gave me some freedom
to see where my comedic mind would take Oda Mae.

Patrick gave me a gift I never got to repay and never
could. Because of him, I got my second Oscar nomination. I never expected to have that opportunity again.
I thought being nominated for *The Color Purple* was a
great experience and that was that. It wouldn't happen
again. And then to find out that I got another nomination . . . I was like, *Okay, here we go.*

I was especially honored to be nominated in the
company of the other women who were up for Best
Supporting Actress: Lorraine Bracco, Diane Ladd, Mary
McDonnell, and Annette Bening. For some reason, the
five of us formed a bond and made a pact together.

We decided that whoever won had to take the other four out on the town. Winner pays all. I think everyone expected that Annette Bening would win that year, so I was incredibly blown over when Denzel Washington announced my name.

My mother wasn't at the ceremony because she didn't want to show disappointment if I lost. My daughter, Alex, and my brother, Clyde, came with me, everyone looking like two million bucks. I spotted the other women seated in their respective seats, and we gave thumbs-ups to each other. Denzel Washington was announcing the supporting actress award. It seemed everyone jumped up almost faster than I did when he called my name.

From the podium, I could see the other four women all hooting and hollering for me. And for the first time, I felt like I was in with my peers. It was a good feeling.

That night, following the ceremony, I was at a party at Spago hosted by superagent Swifty Lazar and his wife, Mary, surrounded by all the famous people who made all the movies I had watched for most of my life. They were all the reasons I wanted to be an actor. There I was, in the same room with all these people whom I had just been enamored with most of my life.

I met all of these actors and directors who said,

"Listen, anytime you want to talk, give us a call." And they gave me their phone numbers.

Billy Wilder, the famous director of movies like *Some Like It Hot*, *The Apartment*, and *Sabrina*, was there with his wife, and they were like, "Come sit with us. Tell us about you." Billy and I talked about movies for an hour. I kept thinking about all the stars I had met between *The Color Purple* and *Ghost*—Gregory Peck, Jack Lemmon, Sophia Loren, and Elizabeth Taylor.

Now here is one of those crazy things where I could really use my mother's memory. For some reason, I think I first met Elizabeth Taylor at some fundraiser, where we were seated at the same table with our mothers. I think that was when ET asked if I could be part of a fundraiser she was doing. She said, "Before you say anything, just know that many, many people have turned me down. It's to raise money for people with AIDS." She had me at "fundraiser," so I just kept saying yes until she heard me say, "YES." I explained that I'd been living in Berkeley when the AIDS plague hit and that I had no problem doing whatever I could to combat it.

But I have another ET memory, which starts crazy mostly because I still can't remember why I got invited. I was at Tiffany's, one of my favorite places, for a book launch for Carole Bayer Sager, who I didn't really know.

But I went because, come on, I'm from the projects and Tiffany's is not a place I ever thought I would be hanging out in, eating little hors d'oeuvres while waiting for someone to say, "EMPTY YOUR POCKETS!" Anyway, I was standing around looking lost, trying to figure out WTF I was really doing there, when I heard, "Psst."

I looked around and saw ET. She waved, and I looked away because I was trying (a) not to stare and (b) not to freak out because it was ET.

Again, I heard, "Psst."

I turned, and she was waving me over to her. She said something like, "Didn't you hear me *psst*-ing at you?"

And I was like, "Yeah."

"Did you not see me waving at you?"

I said, "Yes, but I didn't think you actually were waving at me."

For some reason, she said, "Why not?"

I said, "Because YOU are a big-ass movie star."

And she said, "Well, hell, so are you!"

Yeah, she made me feel really great. Then she said, "You did the benefit for me. By the way, how's your mother?"

"She's great," I said. "I'll tell her you asked for her." I did the same, asking about her mom. She asked me about my life, who was managing me, and I told her.

Then she gave me some sage advice. "You want to get a gift from the studio every time you work," she told me.

"What do you mean?"

"Listen, I ask for a present for every film I do, something I can remember my career by," she told me. "You're going to put all these agents' and managers' kids through private high schools and the best colleges. You're going to pay for the plastic surgery for the different faces of their various wives. Because of your career, you are going to take care of a lot of people. So ask for a nice gift in return. Don't be piggy about it, but it's okay to ask for it."

I listened to her, especially when she said, "A career goes up and down like this." She waved her hand like the dips and peaks of a roller coaster. "Your career is going to be a little different because you are black. You should have something that will remind you in the hard times that you were an actor in films. Something that you can look over at and say in ten or fifteen years, 'Yeah, I was here. I know because these guys gave me this piece of art, or this jewelry, for doing this movie.' It doesn't have to be something ridiculous in price. Just enough. It doesn't hurt anybody. It comes out of their budget." I pointed out that that might work if you're Elizabeth Taylor. But she was right, and she fought for everything she ever got her whole career. She made it part of her contract. She gave a lot and expected something to keep.

So that's what my agents and managers did for me. I currently have my art collection and a lot of the things I have because ET told me they would be a chronicle of my career. I can now look at a painting and remember that it was given to me for doing a specific movie. I still think she had something to do with the studios all saying yes.

Elizabeth Taylor was an inspiration to me, not only as an actor but as a humanitarian and as a woman. She took many slings and arrows from people about her weight, her marriages, and her illnesses, even her name. She did not like it when people called her Liz. She never let that crap get in the way. And that Dame—you know she was DAME Elizabeth Taylor. But she didn't rub it in your face.

She was smart. I looked at her political influence when she showed up for something. She was the best example of what fame could do to help people. Long before they were even certain how AIDS was contracted, when it was still being called "the gay plague," ET had the balls to get involved and, in essence, forced President Ronald Reagan to take notice and take action. Unlike today, when many celebs sign on to be spokespersons for LGBTQ+ issues, back then people were scared for the most part. Certainly, no one of ET's caliber was in that arena in the early days of the AIDS battle in the 1980s. I'm sure her agents and advisers told her to choose a different cause than HIV and AIDS, to let someone else do it. She said, "I'm doing this because I am watching as people I love and have worked with in over fifty films—friends, actors, hair and makeup people, musicians, dancers, some of the most important and influential people—are being alienated and tossed out of their families and communities, being left alone to die on their own. Who gives a goddamn about careers," she told them, "when the people without whom we wouldn't have a career are dying?"

I respected the hell out of that.

Elizabeth Taylor made me feel like I belonged.

The other time I felt that way was my second Oscar nom, especially after meeting the other four women nominated in the Best Supporting Actress category that year.

We all met at the Oscar Nominees Luncheon. We were seated at the same table, and it turned out that we were all a bunch of great dames—Annette, Mary, Diane, Lorraine, and me. We all made a pact that whoever won owed everyone else at the table an elaborate lunch. I won that year, and I was off to the races. No one is allowed to replicate the image of the Oscar statue, but I called somebody on the committee and explained that I needed to make four Oscars out of chocolate, covered in gold foil, to give to the other actresses, and why. They agreed to this one-time thing. So when I took the women out, a chocolate Oscar was at each of their places at the table.

I felt like the five of us women had our arms around each other. I loved meeting them and spending time with them. We all felt the same. We wanted to be there for each other, celebrate when any of us were succeeding, and hold our arms out to catch each other when we fell.

In the early 1980s, Helen Gurley Brown, an editor at *Cosmopolitan* magazine, launched the idea that women could "have it all": an important job, success, great sex, a meaningful marriage, children, and self-care to look great and feel great. Women have been trying to make that happen ever since.

I say, you can have it all. But you've got to walk away from the idea that it's going to look like some movie. Having it all is as messy as you can get. You're going to have consequences for your choices. Not everybody is going to think you've got it together. That's the hard part of that kind of goal. You're going to spend your life trying to figure it out. There are going to be really great times when you feel like what you do matters. And then there will be times when you have to accept that you aren't all that and you have to rely on other people for help, like I did with my mother when I asked for her help raising my daughter.

One time, I was at my home in Berkeley for a while. My mom and Alex lived in the house at the front of the property. Because I get up and down for half the night, I'd usually spend the night in the back house when I was there. One night, when Alex was close to fourteen, I looked out the window and saw her sneaking out of the front house to go hang out with friends after 10:00 p.m.

I decided to lock all the doors so she couldn't get back in, so she'd understand that she had been caught and there would be consequences. I kept a watch for her. A couple hours later, she was out on the porch, knowing she couldn't knock on the door and give herself up. She sat there, waiting.

My mother opened the front door and said to Alex, "What are you doing out here?"

By this time, I had come around to the front, and I said, "Ask her again. Ask her why she's out here instead of in her bedroom."

Ma said, "What happened?"

Alex was completely silent, looking at me like only a pissed-off teenager can.

Since she wasn't talking, I got a bit puffed up. "Well, she snuck out of the house. That's what happened. That's why she's sitting out here. She couldn't get back in."

I thought my mother was going to speak to Alex about her choices. Instead, she turned to me, crossing her arms, and said, "And this is what you're all giddy about?"

Alex hid her smile with her hand.

I said, "You know what? I'm just gonna keep my mouth shut now. I'm going back to the other house. I'll be there. Then I'm going off to do what I need to do."

I wasn't mad. I think my mom was putting it in order. She knew Alex wasn't going to respond to my approach.

Later on, Alex said that her granny had sat her down in the house after I left and said, "Listen, I can tell you not to do this a million times. But it's not until it's going to be unfortunate for you, and something happens, that you'll hear me. Be smarter than that."

I guess it worked . . . for a while.

My mom had a point. That's what it is with teenagers. I thought I knew it all, too, when I was fourteen. I didn't change certain things until it became unfortunate for me. And I was over thirty. You'd think I would have been smarter than that. But we get there when we get there. Hopefully alive.

Yeah, I would never win a mother award. Alex knows now why it was the way it was, especially since she's raised three kids of her own. Because "having it all" is fucking messy, and you've got to own it.

I had to say to Alex, "Look, this is what I'm going to do. I'm going to go to work. And I'm doing it so that you, me, Granny, and Uncle Clyde can have a different life."

I still know that explanations don't really fly when you're a kid. You want your mom. I haven't been a kid for a long, long time, and I still want my mom.

Often I'll hear from another performer or an actor like Jennifer Hudson or a comedian like Jo Koy that I influenced them as kids. Sometimes people will tell me that they saw my Broadway show on HBO or saw me on *Comic Relief* or in a movie when they were kids. Younger people will come up to me at events or even on the street and tell me that seeing me do my thing made them feel like there was a place for them, too. That makes me feel good, of course. I never set out to be a role model, but I'm grateful that I somehow helped to raise a whole lot of young folks to be true to themselves, to who they are and what they wanted to become.

Chapter Thirteen

I got presented with a baby for my thirty-fourth birthday. My kid had her firstborn daughter, Amara, on November 13, 1989, and turned me into a grandmother. Most moms get a wallet or a necklace for their birthday from their teenage daughters. I got a granddaughter.

I had raised Alex to be able to tell me anything. Her relationship with me was that she didn't hide stuff. If something was going on, she'd tell me. So, one day Alex called to say that she was expecting a baby, that she was pregnant. Then she told me that she wanted to keep it.

I asked her, "Are you sure? You have to be absolutely sure."

She said, "Yes. I want to have this baby. And this baby will love me, and she won't know you." Now to some that may sound harsh, but I understood. See, people would move my kid out of the way and not even realize they had done it. After a while, it really pissed her off. At dinner out, people would just sit down and want a picture, and that pissed everyone off.

So all I could say was, "Okay . . ."

As soon as I could, I called my mother. I said, "This is what's happening. Alex is pregnant, and she wants to keep the baby. I asked her if she's sure, and she said yes. God damn it! . . . Fuck!"

My mother was quiet for about ten seconds. Then, she said, "Okay. So, why is this a problem?"

"What? Why is this a problem? Because Alex has to go to school. She needs to graduate. She should be doing teen stuff. This is going to change her whole life."

"Oh . . . okay. I see," my mother said.

"Wait! What do you see? What do you mean?"

"Well, I see you out there going to Washington, DC, and marching with thousands of other women for choice. I didn't realize you were just marching only for your choice, for what you would choose."

"What! Wait, that's not what—"

She continued, "The truth of the matter is, if this is her choice, it's *her* choice. You know, I'm here. There are enough of us here to help her do this if she decides she wants to keep her baby. Because Alex has a choice, which you are always marching for."

I had no way to reply to that. "Listen," I said. "I'm getting off the phone now, and I'll have to call you later. I'll call you back."

When it was time, my mother went into the delivery room with my kid, who, being fifteen and completely healthy, gave birth to her beautiful, healthy baby girl about two hours later. And when they brought the baby home, my mom knew exactly what to do. She'd been a pediatric nurse, so she knew what she was doing and handled it all without a problem. Just like she said she would.

Years later, Alexandrea told me that she thinks she got pregnant as a teenager because she wanted one person in her life who didn't know who Whoopi Goldberg was.

I thought she was getting her revenge on me for being gone so much. I got it.

There was no way to predict what my mother would say or do in any given situation. Her opinions were authentic to her. She was a singular person. My brother, Clyde, was one, too. That's how Clyde and I were because our mother was our role model. And my mom admired and respected other singular people. She saw no issue in staying singular either.

I married three times before realizing I was better off being singular full-time.

At one of my weddings, my mother said to me, "You know, there's a car out back."

"Is this a car you drive?"

She moved me to the side to talk to me privately. "You know I don't drive."

"I know. Why are you telling me about a car in the back?"

"You don't have to do this. Get married."

I said, "I know I don't. But I've involved other people. I said yes to the proposal when I should have ducked or dove to the left or right. And now all these people have shown up to celebrate."

"Well, you can just get in the car. I will explain to everyone."

"Ma, I can't. I think that would be such a horrific thing to do to the guy."

"Okay," she said.

My mom knew I wasn't in love with this man. I was attached to the idea of being in love, but this wasn't it.

When that marriage went toes up, I thought maybe I just wasn't doing it right.

When I headed into number three, my mother said,

"For God's sake, Caryn, why don't you just have a party instead?"

I should have listened to that sage advice, but I didn't. And when that one ended a couple years later, I told her she was right.

She said, "You have to say to the next one who asks, 'No, I don't think I want to be married.'"

"Okay," I said. "Because I don't like, and I really am not good at, this marriage stuff."

"Then stop doing it. If you're not good at it, stick to the shit you're good at. If you're not good at relationships, stick to being a really good friend to someone. You don't have to live with anyone. You don't have to marry everyone or anyone."

It took me a long time to figure out it was also cheaper to "just have a party instead."

And now, at this age, I don't even bother with a party. Who needs the aggravation? It's all about a "hit and run," and I have them only with someone who completely understands that this is only a "hit and run." I don't even want to have to toss empty beer bottles in the recycle bin after somebody hung out too long. I don't need anybody to stick around after that at all.

The only people, besides my kid and her family, that I could have hung out with all the time were Mom and

Clyde, which is why, once my career was moving ahead, I asked Clyde to be my driver.

After I got famous, when I would go to film a movie, the producers would set me up with a car and a driver to take me back and forth to the set. Then I made a movie called *The Long Walk Home*, which was filmed in Alabama. Clyde was living in Montgomery at the time, working for AT&T.

I was like, "Dude, do you want to drive me? Come on the crew as my driver on the set?"

He told me, "I can't. I work all day for the phone company."

I wanted to take the load off my brother and get him to come back to California with me because I just didn't feel like he was okay being in Alabama.

We started hanging out in the evenings after filming. I said, "Are you sure you want to stay down here? This is quite a different place to live."

"No. I'd love to come to California, but I have to make it happen."

That's when I made my deal with him because I knew it would help me out and it would help Ma, too.

"I will take care of you and Ma if you take care of Ma, especially since she doesn't drive. In the meantime, you can be my driver for movies. Then we can hang out together. We can all be together."

I knew he loved driving. He would make long cross-country road trips whenever he could. I loved Porsche cars, and he was happy to get behind the wheel of one of those.

That's what we agreed to do. I felt better knowing my brother would be with our mom. And as my driver, I knew he always had my back. He understood the difference between Whoopi Goldberg, the personality, and Sis.

Everybody on the sets loved him because he was so fun to be around. Having him around me on movie sets made a huge difference for me because he could read my face and know where I was at.

Whenever he drove me somewhere, he'd say, "Let me go in first and see what's going down."

Sometimes, he'd come back to the car and say, "I don't think you really want to do this. Because there's a lot of stuff going on and a lot of people, and you know, maybe you want to sit this one out."

I'd say, "Okay, cool. I appreciate that."

He was my ace in the hole. He loved going on adventures. Wherever I had to be, he'd be willing to go. And he liked the benefit of being with me, too. It was like him getting to show up places with a puppy.

We'd go somewhere, and an attractive woman would come up to meet me or get my autograph. I'd introduce Clyde as my brother. Being as handsome as he was, the woman would stay and chat him up. The next thing I'd know, he'd be going out later with her.

Like my mother, Clyde loved meeting and talking to actors and performers he admired. They both loved the type of performers who were singular people.

My mom always told me to pay attention to Sammy Davis Jr. She felt he didn't get the recognition he deserved, considering his versatility. She told me he was a rare performer who could do it all. She felt the same way about Michael Jackson. She admired Quincy Jones for his ability to recognize and produce talent in all different types of music. She was a lifelong fan of Judy Garland, Harry Belafonte, and Billie Holiday. She appreciated the unique talents of Freddie Mercury and David Bowie.

In the film world, she admired the actors who held the films together because their performances were always strong.

One day, in the early '90s, I was in California, at my house in the Pacific Palisades, and my mom and my brother were staying there with me for a while.

I got a call from my agent, who told me, "Marlon Brando wants to talk to you."

I thought he was bullshitting me, so I was like, "Yeah, right. Okay."

My agent said, "No, really. Marlon Brando wants to call you. He likes you a lot and wants to know you as a friend."

"You're serious then? Okay. Sure. Give him the number."

Clyde and my mom were both out doing something together, so it was just me and the housekeeper at the house.

About forty minutes later, my phone rang, and I said, "Hello." And I hear this voice I know because I've watched every movie he's been in, some of them many times. I stood there with my phone up to my ear, grinning.

He said, "Well, I would like to sit down and talk to you. Can we do that, you know, on Thursday or sometime soon?"

I said, "Okay. Do you want to come here? Or I can come to you."

And Marlon said, "No. I will come see you."

So I gave him the address, and we both hung up. I was pretty sure my mom and brother were going to be thrilled about this.

Behind my house was a canyon with a sloping hill

and a garden. I decided to go out and cut some flowers for a vase. I was out there with my clippers when I heard my piano being played. I wasn't sure why I was hearing music because I knew the housekeeper didn't play piano and no one else was home. So, I got a little freaked out, thinking some stranger had found his way in.

I tiptoed around the back of the house and grabbed a long garden tool, something I could hit somebody with if I had to. I eased the french doors open and looked in. It was Marlon Brando playing my piano. He was playing the song "Stardust." I was standing there with a shovel handle in my hand thinking, *Marlon Brando is playing piano in my house!* I'm sure my mouth was hanging open.

He didn't stop playing.

When he finished, I said, "That was amazing, but what are you doing here? I thought we were meeting on Thursday."

He said, "Well, we had such a good conversation, I decided I was going to come over right away. The housekeeper let me in."

"Okay. Are you hungry? Can I get you something to eat or drink?"

He didn't want anything, so I took him to the living room. I knew there was no way for me to prepare my mother or brother to let them know that Marlon Brando was in the house. (This was about five years before cell phones.)

First, we started talking about an acting class he was teaching, and he wanted me to make a special appearance and talk to the students. Then, we got to talking about films we loved.

About thirty minutes into our conversation, my mother came through the front door.

I said, "Ma, let me introduce you to *Marlon Brando*."

She stopped in her tracks, and I saw her eyes light up like they were on fire. It was like her hair grew five inches and became illuminated. She walked toward us like the Queen of Sheba. She extended her hand very formally, and her voice got husky and sultry as she said, "It's a pleasure to meet you, Mr. Brando. You must know that I'm a very big fan of your work."

I was looking at her like she was this stranger I hadn't seen since she met Sidney Poitier. That same person had shown up, again, for Marlon Brando. She turned into this sexpot before my eyes.

Marlon stood up, leaned over, and kissed her on the hand as he held it.

Now my mother's head was about to explode.

Marlon said to her, "You are stunning. Your daughter

and I have been talking about movies. And I'm pleased to meet you now."

She smiled demurely. "Well, I'm going to go upstairs now. Again, Mr. Brando, a pleasure." She turned and sauntered toward the staircase.

I was thinking, *Really, Ma?* But I was trying not to laugh.

A little while later, my brother came in.

And I said, "Clyde, I want you to say hello to *Marlon Brando.*"

Clyde walked over to Marlon, who stood back up, and they hugged and then did a series of hand-slapping handshakes like they had rehearsed them.

I was watching all of this thinking, *Do you even know that you're talking to Marlon Brando? Because you guys are acting like you've been on the street together for years.*

Then Clyde said to Marlon, "You know, it's been really cool talking to you. I'm glad I got to see you." They repeated the whole hand-slapping handshake thing, and my brother went upstairs.

Marlon stayed for another thirty minutes to talk to me about his island in Fiji and his efforts to preserve the ecosystem. He was also into growing spirulina and algae in the ocean that could be dried and used as high-protein food to feed people around the world.

After he left, my mother and brother came down the stairs like two little kids on Christmas morning. They were waving their hands in the air and screaming, "Oh, my God. Oh, my God. Marlon Brando was in this house!"

We all started dancing around and shimmying. We were doing all kinds of crazy stuff.

My brother said to me, "God damn, I guess you're famous."

I was laughing my ass off and said, "I think so, too. It must be."

That was the first day of my ongoing friendship with Marlon Brando.

When he passed away, I got a phone call that he had left me a parcel of land on his Fiji island. It really threw me for a loop. I never expected that.

A while later, an attorney for the family called me and said, "I know Marlon left you a part of the island, but we'd like to ask you to give it back because if everybody keeps theirs, there won't be an island left."

I told them that I understood and that I wanted to have it go back to Marlon's family.

The only other time I really saw Ma's coy Sidney Poitier–Marlon Brando personality come out again was when she went with me to the White House. I did some work for Bill Clinton's presidential campaign for both terms. I found out that she also had a good friend working for Clinton's campaign.

I said, "Ma, the president is coming in, and I'm going to be at this event for him. Do you want to go with me and meet him?"

She very nonchalantly said, "Okay. Sure."

So I took my mother with me to the White House for a big fundraiser for the second term. I was standing there in a crowded room with her, and Ma's friend on the campaign came over and gave her a big hug. Then the doors swung open, and in came Bill Clinton.

It's no secret that he just has that thing, that crazy sex appeal women like when they go near him. It was talked about all the time.

Bill came over to say hello, and he leaned over my mother, took her hand, and said with that southern drawl, "I'm so pleased to meet Whoopi's mother."

Before my eyes, my mother turned into a twenty-five-year-old. She looked like one of those paintings from the '60s of black women with Afros. She was glowing, like sparks of light were bouncing off her head.

Her voice dropped down all husky and quiet, and she said, "Oh. Oh, Mr. President."

He stayed and talked with her for about ten

minutes, and it was amazing for me to see, to watch my mother chatting with a US president, something I'm sure she never thought she would do. My mother appreciated his loyalty and conviction about the Head Start programs. He was strong about it all eight years. Mom always felt that children were not being respected enough and that the government needed to put some more programs like Head Start out there for the public. Like President Clinton, she believed very strongly that if you can give a kid a head start, they have a much better possibility of succeeding.

Watching my mom with him made me realize how magical my life actually has been.

When Barack Obama was elected our forty-fourth president, she said to me, "Well, I never thought I'd see this day. A black president in the White House. I never ever thought this day would ever come."

Clyde had the same thing going on for him as Bill Clinton when it came to women. Women would fall out of the sky when Clyde was around. If he met you, he'd probably stay in touch with you. He also went to the neighborhood reunions and kept in touch with everybody in the neighborhood.

When my brother died of a brain aneurysm in 2015,

we had three memorial services: one in Berkeley, one in Los Angeles, and one in New York.

At the first memorial in Berkeley, two women came up to talk to me at different times. One said, "I don't know if you know this, but Clyde and I had plans to live together." The other said, "Clyde and I were going to drive to New York and visit you in a month." They were both crying and carrying on.

Then, we went to do a memorial in Los Angeles. I was standing with Alex when she said, "Here comes another one."

Sure enough, two other women approached us separately to say, "Clyde and I planned to move in together," or "Clyde was planning to take me with him here or there."

Alex started to side-eye me, and later she asked, "How many women was he seeing?"

I had no idea, but in my head, I was saying to him, "Good God, Clyde. This shit is crazy ridiculous."

When we got to New York, the story repeated itself with a couple of other women. Each woman looked different from the others—different hues, colors, languages, ages, sizes, it didn't matter.

I swear, by the time the New York memorial was over, I could hear my brother chuckling in my soul. Women loved my brother, but he had no intention of settling down with any of them. He was a man of the world. He loved to dress like a king, drive beautiful cars, and have a good time. He was quite something.

About a year after he passed, I had a dream about my brother. I'm standing, wearing a backpack. And I'm at school, like my grammar school, and I'm wearing a school uniform. Clyde comes walking up, and I'm thinking to myself, *Look at you standing there like that. How are you doing?* Then, it comes to me. *Wait. You're dead. I better faint.* So I make myself faint.

Clyde leans over me and says, "Why are you fainting?"

"I don't know," I say. "How are you?"

"I'm good. Everything's good. I just want to say hi." Clyde gives me a big hug.

I tell him, "I'll see you soon."

He says, "Not too soon."

And that was that.

In a way, I'm relieved that both Clyde and my ma passed away before number forty-five got to have his one term in office. I know my mom would be so discouraged at how his attitude turned people against each other, how women's rights got reversed, and how much worse it started looking for black folks and other people of color in this country.

When I was a little kid in the projects, I would see old ladies who had numbers stamped on their arms. I didn't know what it was then but came to understand it later in life. When I got older and had conversations with these elderly Jewish women who had survived the atrocities of the Holocaust, they said to me, "Keep your eyes very peeled. Because it's never happened here in the US, but it doesn't mean that it can't. When you hear things that don't sound good being brought up around you, you need to listen. And when these things start happening and you start losing your rights as an American, then you have to really prick up your ears."

One of the ladies told me, "You don't want to be caught like we were. We didn't get out in time. We didn't get out fast enough."

Since 2016, that's been on my mind. I'm listening. I'm watching. And I've got things prepared should anything get worse. But it would make my mom and brother enraged and sad that America has taken such a big step backward.

I still have hope, and I know most people in this country just want to live their own lives and keep the peace, but I'm listening and watching very closely.

Chapter Fourteen

Certain things transport me to my mom. I'll catch a scent in the air or taste something that brings her to me, even now.

If someone comes around me with a bag of Wise potato chips, especially the onion-garlic flavor, it takes me to being with my mom. The same is true of Werther's butterscotch candy, Jean Nate bath powder, and Chanel No. 5 perfume. Those things never make me feel sad; they're mostly good memories.

However, every time I hear the song "Who Can I Turn To?" I get teary-eyed. It was written by two British composers, Leslie Bricusse and Anthony Newley, and probably the most famous recording was by Tony Bennett in the mid-1960s. My mom would always sing along with the record.

The lyrics feel like they sum up my mom and how she made her way through life, and in some ways, it's where I'm at now, too. It's about feeling like you lost your guiding star and now you're wondering who you're going to turn to, who will understand you.

I've never been depressed. Or if I have, I didn't recognize it. Once again, I'm lucky that way. I can see it in some family members, though. As much as my mother loved her life in California and having her house and garden, along with my dogs and cats, who were all devoted to her, there was a darkness that would surround her once in a while. Sometimes when I'd look over at her, she was not there except physically. She would be in some different place, probably a memory I had no part of, one that she was never going to talk about. I'd wait, let her be, not talk to her, and after a couple minutes, she would be back. I guess history had snuck up on her uninvited, and there was no point in letting it stay.

I didn't know anything about feeling lost until after she died. I wouldn't call it crippling grief because it doesn't have a grip on me. It is more of a grief that stays way down in my toes. It doesn't feel dark. It's a kind of fog or numbness. I can't figure out what I'm supposed to feel now. I'm not raving angry, but I resent the fact that my mom and Clyde aren't here anymore.

It's not like either one could have done anything about dying, but from time to time, I feel like, *Why did y'all leave me here?*

I'm not in any rush to go wherever they went, but a lot of days, I'm just sort of walking through it, getting where I need to go and doing what I need to do. I had no clue that things would change so dramatically for me once they were gone. Was I so tethered to my mom and brother that I can't find my own bearings? It feels that way. They were my home base, my reality check, because they both knew me from the start.

A couple months before my mother passed, I apologized to her.

"Ma, I'm sorry I was such an asshole sometimes when I was a kid."

She shook her head and smiled at me. "All kids are assholes at some point. It's part of what you're supposed to be. You have to get to know what's going to work out for you and what isn't."

"Okay," I said. "But was it really, really hard to get through?"

"No," she told me, "because I knew what was coming. When you have children, then you have to expect that they're going to be different from you. But the differences aren't in every way." She waited for a minute and then said, "I looked in the mirror one day, and I saw my mother coming out of my shirt. Same will happen to you. One day you'll look and see me coming out of your shirt."

She knew what would happen. More and more, I'm starting to look like her and sound like her. I look in the mirror, and there's my mom . . . coming out of my shirt.

It doesn't bother me, except I want her to still be here. I need my mom. I still need her to tell me, "Check your face" when I host *The View*. She used to watch the show and then call me and tell me that my face looked like I was not having any of whatever a guest or one of the other hosts was saying. She would tell me that my face was showing it all, and it wasn't good. My daughter does it for me now.

"It looks like you're pissed off or not agreeing at all, and I don't think that's what you want people to see because it might not be true."

She was right.

That's really the thing that I got from my mom while I was growing up: to be kind to people even when you don't like them or agree with what they're saying.

She would always say, "It doesn't take much to be kind. There are things you can do. You can be kind with no money."

Even early on in my career, she made me understand that I had a responsibility to be kind to my fans. She would remind me that it probably took a lot for a person to walk up and ask me for an autograph.

She would tell me, "When you're here at home, you're just you. But when you go out the door, they're expecting Whoopi Goldberg. So do your best. And if you're on your period, don't go outside. Don't go anywhere because you're a little tough when you have your period."

My mom and brother were the only ones who could tell me, "Don't be a dick," and it would feel like love. Because it was.

She could say anything to me, and I could say things to her that I couldn't really say to other people. She could hear beyond my words when I was talking to her. She understood what was happening for me. To a similar extent, my brother was the same way.

As I walk into my sixty-ninth year on earth, I'm thinking to myself, *Now, this is what becomes a legacy, right? My mom and brother left me enough information to get through however long I have left here.*

I know I'm okay on my own, but I didn't really know how lost I would feel. I stopped moving around much after my mom passed. I didn't really want to go out to the theater, or concerts, or Yankees games, or basketball games. I used to have parties at the house. I didn't want to have anyone over. But I did make an effort. I knew my mom would want my brother and me to keep on celebrating birthdays and holidays and having a good time even if she wasn't here.

Then when Clyde passed away, I thought, *Now what?* I had a hard time feeling up to doing much at all. Clyde was my beacon. He was the one person left who knew everything about me. He knew everything about our mom. He was my port in the storm as a kid when she was hospitalized. And he gave me peace of mind when I was older and he was looking after her. When he passed away, I really lost my footing. I felt very scattered.

It was the first time I felt like an adult, totally on my own. Before, I was always my mother's kid and my brother's little sister. Now I was only a stand-alone adult. I didn't know how to be. I wasn't prepared not to have anyone older than me.

I would want to come home from work and just roll up and hibernate. But I knew I couldn't do that. I knew if I slipped into letting grief immobilize me, I could swim around in it for a long time. I really didn't want to get like that. The way I was raised is that you pull yourself together. And if you can't, then you need to ask for help.

You have to talk to someone about it. It has happened a couple times for me since she died. I've had to talk to somebody about what was happening to me.

I knew what my mother would have said if I had given in to closing out the world. I can hear her in my head: "Get off the bed. Get up and go do something. Do something meaningful. You're still alive, you know? It can't be about me not being there. It can't be about your brother not being there. This is about how you're still there. What are you going to do?"

I had to show up for my work and project commitments. I had to be okay for my daughter and her family.

I've started writing cards to my friends who are now going through it and have recently lost their own mom. I want to pass along to them what I found out for myself, hoping it will help. Maybe it can be helpful to you, too.

I start out by saying that other people who still have their moms will not know what to do or how to respond to your loss. Do your best to be kind to them even when you're not feeling it.

There will be times when people who haven't lost a parent, particularly their mother, are going to say things to you that make you think, *What the fuck! You don't know what you are talking about.* They aren't where you're at. They don't know any better. The best you can do is say, "Thank you," then wrap it up quickly and get the hell away.

There will be people you like a lot, even other family members, who are talking to you, and you'll realize you're just not there with them. You checked out and didn't hear whatever they were saying. That's okay. It's going to go like that.

The loss of your mom is the loss of the first person who ever looked at you and thought, *This is my baby.* Regardless of whether she raised you all the way through, you were still a part of her in the beginning. She was the first person who looked at you and thought, *Okay, wow. Here we go.*

If you were put in the arms of a woman who took it on herself to be your mom, that's the person who made sure you stayed alive. She fed you. You peed on her. You threw up on her. And she still took care of you, talked to you, and got you to the point where you could do more for yourself. So she was the first connection in your life. When you're a kid, you never think about that relationship coming to an end. Even as you get older, you don't let your mind fully accept that she's not going to be there someday.

For those of us who have lost our mom, our grief is going to be different from one another's. A lot of folks might go into deep mourning right after losing their mom. For some of us, it takes a while to feel it. An anomaly about me is that it took a long time for her loss to really set in on me. I put the grief in a compartment because I'm an efficient person. I wanted to get shit done, do what needed to happen, and figure out how to get through it. But that's not how it goes.

If you mourn right away or try to put it on hold, or can't really feel much at all, there is still one thing we all have in common. There's no timeline and no finite ending to grief for your mom. You keep waiting for it to change or to feel differently.

Some days the tears are going to come, and you just have to let that be. They might not be convenient, or they might show up unexpectedly. If you go into a funk, then really let yourself go fully into it. Pull up a fainting chair. Draw the curtains. Close out the world for a while and get as insane in your grief as you ever thought you could. Get into an insanity funk all over the house. Let it out. It will help you get up faster and back into life.

But count on the grief to come back. Even years later. Three years after my mom passed, I would sometimes think, *Why am I still feeling like this?*

It's not a grief that has an end date. It evolves, but it stays around. You know, it becomes something that hangs out in the corner. It's still nearby, every day. And sometimes it comes up and runs at you. You just have to let it do what it's going to do.

If it's uncomfortable for you, don't put yourself in places where people might be celebrating and having a good time. At first, being around other people who are out there getting on with life might make you feel somewhat angry. Again, they aren't going through it. You have to remember that you're looking at it all through the eyes of loss.

Eventually, you have to separate your grief for your mom and your grief for yourself. That's okay, too, but you have to call it what it is. If you're grieving for yourself for a long time, get some help from somebody who can help you figure it out. Take the onus off it. You're not crazy; you only need to talk some stuff out.

My best advice to anybody who has lost their mom is to find a way to celebrate her life. Regardless of what your relationship was with her, figure out how to find some humor in who she was and your life with her.

The best way to honor your mom is to laugh.

Laughing makes you breathe differently and lightens everything up so you can see where you're going and put one foot in front of the other. I was so fortunate to be my mother's daughter and my brother's sister. I got to be with people who knew how to have a good time when they could. We had a good time when I was a kid, and there wasn't even extra money to eat out at a nice restaurant or take an actual vacation away from New York. We made up our own good time. I don't know how my mom did it, but I never felt I had to settle for less.

The three of us knew how to enjoy life when it was all going great and I was making enough money for us to do whatever we wanted. We may have upped the experience—Hawaii hotels and spas, trips to London to stay at the Savoy, courtside seats at NBA games, Las Vegas suites and carefree gambling—but it never changed the dynamic among the three of us. We didn't have a good time because there was more money to be had. We could laugh together with whatever was going on. It didn't matter if it was a three-star Michelin restaurant in Rome or a Nathan's hot dog on Coney Island. It was always amazing to go to great places, but it wasn't really about the surroundings. It was about this nucleus family of mine.

I'm lonely, but not for other people. I've got plenty of people in my life: friends, coworkers, and family. I have my daughter and her family. But it's different. Alex has her cocoon of her husband, three kids, and granddaughter. She's got a strong hexagon family of her own making. I'm always included, but it's still not the same. I'm lonely for those people who knew me from my first breath: my mom and my brother.

For those of you who still have your mom, dad, and siblings, don't let a lot of time pass without talking about death. I know it's something we all avoid thinking about, especially in the US, so we're all unprepared for how to handle it. We've hidden it away in sterilized situations, in places where most of us don't go often unless we have to be there. Our family members often die in emergency rooms or during surgery or in the intensive care unit. If they are old or sick, they might be in the hospital or a nursing home, or we might have hospice to help us, which is a godsend. But most of us don't have to face or think about death all that much. Let me tell you when you don't want to have to figure it out: after the person has died.

It's important to have the talk with each other and make sure it's all down on paper, what you want to happen to you, what they want to happen to them. Have the discussion at age twenty-five, then again ten years later, and then another ten years down the road. Make sure that everybody's wishes are up to date.

Maybe you feel estranged from your family, or you have very different views on a lot of things that matter to you. Still, the time to process all of that is while they're alive. Say what you need to say while people can still hear it. Give them a chance to understand and to respond.

Maybe your parent was not motherly at all or particularly kind. Even if they couldn't be a mother or father, they were still a touchstone for you. So, at some point, you'll have to come to terms with your relationship with them. While you can still connect with them, tell them how it is for you and see if they will sit down and talk to you about it. Because once they're gone, that begins to run up on you, the fact that you didn't say what you meant to say, you didn't do what you meant to do. Even if you need to tell them how mad you are, you can do that.

I have a friend whose mom is going through dementia and forgetting a lot. As it progresses, she's becoming a pleasant person everybody loves to be around. This is really different from how she was as a mom.

My friend told me, "Now I can say to her, 'This is how I felt when you did this or that.'"

And her mom looks at her and says, "You know, I'm sorry, dear."

The person she is now is sorry for everything she put her kids through. She doesn't understand when she did it, but she knows she caused her daughter some pain.

My friend said, "I feel like my mother may hear something from time to time."

I said, "Keep it nice so you don't scare her. She can't remember where she is or why she's there. The person you're talking to now isn't the same person she was when you were a little kid."

She told me, "If it had been like this when I was growing up, we would have had a different relationship."

I get what she's saying, but I also remind my friends that it's easy to forget that our parents were kids, and they had parents, too. You don't necessarily know how they were raised. So, you have to be a lot better about opening up to say, "I don't know how you were raised and how it made you the way you are."

Even if you don't get to say it to your mom, at least recognize that she might have responded to you the way her parents responded to her as a little kid. She probably did the best she could with little information. Chances are your mom grew up in a family that never talked about their feelings. Maybe they only had the time to figure out how to keep shelter over their heads and enough food for the day. Or maybe they were raised in a strict household where there was no room for a mistake or even individuality. Take a deeper look. It's all more complicated than we like to think.

Like my mom, I come from the school of thinking, *There is no point in standing here screaming and crying about things being bad because I still have to get shit done. So let me just go get it done. If we've got time, then we'll talk about it all at some point. If not, we'll just have to keep moving forward.*

Probably the most difficult task following the death of your mom or a loved one is to physically dismantle the life they had. After my mom died, my brother and I talked through what to do with all her possessions. I had to be back to work on *The View*, so Clyde assured me he would handle it all. Because one of Clyde's favorite things to do was drive cross-country, he would come to see me in New York or visit family in Los Angeles. I didn't go back to my Berkeley property for a long time.

I'd ask Clyde, "How's it going, sorting through Ma's stuff?"

He'd always say, "I got it. Everything's okay."

It wasn't until Clyde passed away that I figured out that he had not touched one thing in the front house since Ma had died. Nothing had changed in five years.

It made me realize that he couldn't do it on his own. He was so attached to our mother that everything in the house had a sentimental memory for him.

This is the other thing I tell my friends in grief: If

you have siblings, go through all the belongings together. Pick a time when you can be together. You won't know what holds meaning for your brother or sister. You're going to have to get rid of a lot of stuff, but you can at least ask each other, "Anybody want this?"

It's all going to take time. So if you have the option, don't try to do it all at once. Pick days when everybody can participate. Start with the valuable things and then move on to furniture, books, papers, and clothing.

If you're an only child, see if a cousin or a good friend will jump in with you. It's good to have extra people to talk to about memories or silly things you did with your loved one. If someone else helps you with the process, you can run things by them, too: *Keep it? Or let it go?* You'll probably cry some. It's going to be tough because somewhere in the back of your childhood mind, you never thought your mom wouldn't be in that house, that room, that bed. But you'll also laugh if someone else is with you because crying and laughing aren't that far apart in the world of memories.

In the beginning, you might feel like you can barely stand to let anything go. Do what you can to be realistic, but also cut yourself some slack. Box up the stuff you keep and find a place to put it for a year. A year later, go through the boxes. You'll feel less sentimental and more willing to let a lot of it go. After a year, you're going to look around and think, *I've got to get rid of a lot of this.* It's not disrespectful to your loved one that you don't keep everything they had. After a year, keep what means something to you now, whatever that might be.

In the end, I only kept my mom's things that felt like the strongest connection to her.

Somebody asked me recently what I'd do if I could have my mom with me for one more long weekend.

For the first couple of hours, Alex and the grandkids and everyone who loved her so much would be jumping all over her and carrying her everywhere.

Then I'd say, "Come and get in this car with me." I'd want her to experience an electric car because they weren't around in 2010. And I'd show her how far smartphones and technology have come.

Next, I'd say, "Come to Italy with me and see the house I got there." On the flight I would tell her everything that's happened since she left: all the good, the bad, and the strange. We'd go to the beach in Italy, sit in the sun, smoke joints, and just laugh.

As I write these last thoughts about my mom, I'm looking down at my electric-blue metallic fingernail polish. My kid made me get a manicure with her, and now I'm hooked on having shiny nails. My mom had beautiful hands and long, strong fingernails, and she would have loved having all the nail design variety you can get now, the glitter, the symbols, the gems, and the full scope of colors. I'd end up taking her for a manicure. I think she'd choose metallic gold. Yeah, gold for the singular person she was.

Whatever our long weekend would turn out to be, I know she would be appreciative because she was always that way, especially after she came to California. She was very grateful for all the days she didn't have to go to work. She loved the days when she got to travel and not wonder what time she had to be back. She was freed up to enjoy her life.

I never had to wonder if she was happy. Nothing was left unsaid between Mom, Clyde, and me. I know my mission to give back to her everything she had given me happened while she was alive.

I always wanted her to know that she was the best mother for me. She not only gave birth to me, but she gave life to my outlook, my confidence, and my dream. Every November 13, my birthday, I would have flowers sent to my mother with a card that read: "Thanks for letting me rent the room."

She appreciated every gift, every kind gesture, and every opportunity. It didn't matter if she was in the halls of the White House or sitting in a lawn chair in the garden reading a book—it was always a great day to her. She'd call me up and say, "I just want to say thank you. This was a perfect day. I had a great time, a great time."

At other times, she'd say, "I'm so appreciative that Clyde's here with me, and you're there doing what you do, and we're staying together and doing this as a family."

I think that's my new mission: to be more appreciative of my days, like my mom. Because there's no doubt: I am the luckiest person in the world.

Acknowledgments

To Tom Leonardis, James Jahrsdoerfer, Stephanie Suski, Mel Berger, Marcia Wilkie, Josie Woodbridge, and everyone at Blackstone who helped make this possible, and everyone who helped make our lives better (not bitter).